AN ATLAS OF
WORLD AFFAIRS

This remarkably useful and unique reference book supplies basic information on virtually every aspect of contemporary world happenings. More than 70 newly-drawn maps focus on those regions of the world which are in the news. These areas have been singled out for their importance in cold war, hot war, local dispute, or global controversy. The Atlas clarifies each country's vital resources, its finances, populations, alliances and political trends. A succinct, but adequate text accompanies each map, explaining the background and summarizing the situation. A competent index gives a handy cross-reference to related subjects.

Andrew Boyd is assistant editor of the British weekly magazine *The Economist*. The maps were drawn by W. H. Bromage, a member of the staff of the London *News Chronicle*.

'To the reader who wants a quick reference to the phrases and names that occur almost daily in the news media, this volume will prove invaluable'—*Military Review*.

'This will be a most welcome volume in reference collections'—*The Library Journal*.

AN ATLAS OF
WORLD AFFAIRS

ANDREW BOYD

MAPS BY
W. H. BROMAGE

FREDERICK A. PRAEGER *Publishers*

NEW YORK

BOOKS THAT MATTER

*Published in the United States of America in 1959
by Frederick A. Praeger, Inc., Publishers
15 West 47th Street, New York 36, NY*

*Library of Congress catalog card
number: 57-13228*

Printed in Great Britain

Foreword

With all due respect to Mr Edmund Clerihew Bentley, geography is about maps *and* chaps. Men make frontiers, cities—and canals. Men find and exploit oilfields, farmlands, fisheries—and uranium. Men quarrel over these things—and over politics, religion, race, and language; and their quarrels, like their creations, change the map.

Today's map is changing fast. Every nine months, on average, during this generation, a new sovereign state has come into being, vibrant with fresh nationalism. Among older states some have been seeking to forge new links with one another; others have been swallowed up or truncated. A great clash of ideologies overlaps with the jarring readjustment of relations between races, between nations rich and poor, great and small, old and new. Rising populations press upon natural frontiers. Men armed with new techniques push back those frontiers in their search for the wealth hidden in polar wastes and tropical deserts.

Anyone who tries to set down some of the complexities of this changing world in simple form is indebted to the pioneer work of Mr J. F. Horrabin. The admirable simplicity of his pre-war *Atlas of Current Affairs* is hard to emulate nowadays. The post-war nations are more numerous, their affairs more involved and interlinked. But, like Mr Horrabin's, mine is still 'an exercise in the art of leaving out'. Both in the maps, drawn by Mr W. H. Bromage, for whose patient collaboration I am very grateful, and in the text that accompanies them, the aim is to select what is relevant, not to fill in every detail that a normal atlas would provide.

The sources from which I have drawn are too numerous to list, but all reputable; any errors are mine. Cross-references are indicated in the text by an italic numeral in brackets, thus: (*44*). The number refers to a map and its accompanying note, *not* to a page; so do the entries in the index.

A. B.

Note on the Second Edition

Since this book first appeared less than two years ago, the map has changed with the creation of the United Arab Republic, the attaining of independence by Malaya and Guinea, the opening of the six-nation European Common Market, the federating of the West Indies, and many other events. We have heard a lot about sputniks, Atlas ICBMs, Christmas Island and Canaveral; about the 'Rapacki plan', 'disengagement', 'convertibility' and the 'twelve-mile limit'; about the fall of military rulers in Latin America and their rise in Asia. We have been anxious about Lebanon, Iraq, Jordan, Quemoy, Tibet and Berlin. We have seen a great acceleration in African pressure for independence. This thoroughly revised edition deals with all these matters, and seeks also to indicate some of the changes that will come in the months ahead.

A. B.

May 1959

Contents

AN ATLAS OF
WORLD AFFAIRS

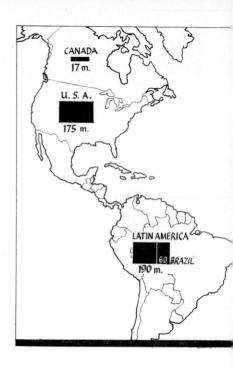

I

PEOPLE

There are now nearly 2,800 million people in the world. Thus the human race has increased in numbers by over half since 1920, when there were about 1,820 million.

Of the three biggest concentrations of people—China and Japan (710 mn.), India and Pakistan (480 mn.), Europe (415 mn.)—the first two are in Asia. Asia as a whole contains, and has probably always contained, over half the world's people. The Asian and African countries, now often called the 'Bandung' countries (*11*), contain nearly two-thirds. The countries usually grouped as 'western'—western Europe, the Americas, and Australasia—contain little over a quarter; but, largely thanks to the United States, they are much the most productive group. Communist governments now control a third of the human race (*8*).

Population growth can be a particularly serious problem in areas where death from disease has been sharply reduced, while custom religion, ignorance or deliberate policy leaves the birth rate unchecked. A high rate of increase can be alarming to a country's

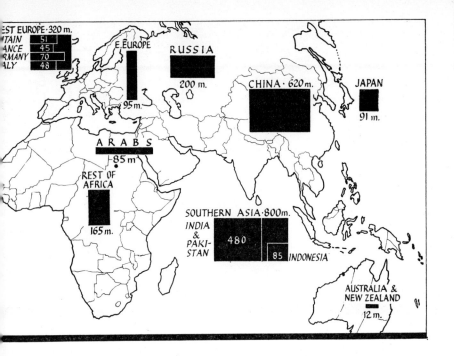

neighbours; for instance, in South-East Asia, where millions of Chinese are already settled (59). In 1959 the Chinese communists, after several shifts in policy, actively favoured a growth of population, as Nazi Germany and Fascist Italy did before the second world war and as Soviet Russia has also done. But attempts to check population growth are being made in India and Japan.

Huge areas are still virtually empty: the jungles of equatorial South America; the desert and semi-desert regions of North Africa, Arabia, Central Asia, and Australia; the Arctic wastelands of Siberia and Canada. New techniques are enabling men to win rich mineral and other resources from some of these areas (38, 45, 60, 65, 69), but they cannot yet be expected to ease the general pressure of population by providing congenial homes and food for great masses of people.

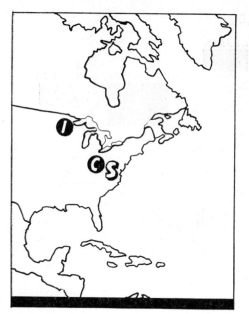

2

POWER

Although atomic energy, oil, and hydro-electric power get most of the headlines today, the bases of the industrial power that determines a country's wealth and often its political power are still coal and iron and steel. Steel is needed to build power plants, oil refineries, and pipelines, as well as ships, railways, bridges, skyscrapers, and factories; coal and iron are needed to produce steel. America and Russia owe their industrial and political predominance largely to their wealth in both coal and iron. In western Europe, the creation in 1951 of a 'coal–steel community' (20) was an attempt to rationalize the natural interdependence of, for example, France's Lorraine iron, Germany's Ruhr coal, and the steelworks of Belgium and Luxemburg, by sweeping aside the national boundaries that divided them.

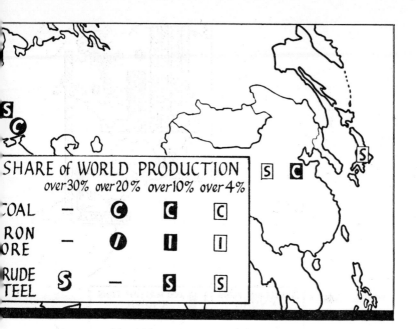

SHARE of WORLD PRODUCTION
over 30% over 20% over 10% over 4%

	over 30%	over 20%	over 10%	over 4%
COAL	—	C	C	C
IRON ORE	—	I	I	I
CRUDE STEEL	S	—	S	S

America, western Europe, and Russia dominate the world in terms of production today. But other regions are certain to increase in importance.

China, since it came under communist rule in 1949, has made particularly strenuous efforts to increase its output of coal and steel. By 1959 it claimed to be producing more steel than Japan, and more coal than Britain. Its reserves of coal are thought to be bigger than Russia's and not far short of America's. Brazil, India, Southern Africa, and Canada each contain huge reserves of iron ore estimated to be larger than those of any of the countries marked on this map.

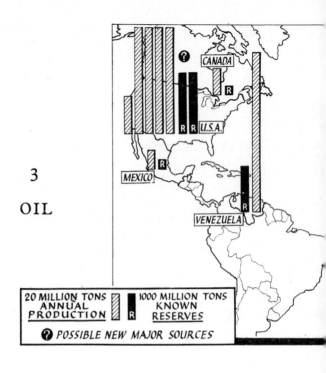

20 MILLION TONS ANNUAL PRODUCTION | 1000 MILLION TONS KNOWN RESERVES R

? POSSIBLE NEW MAJOR SOURCES

3

OIL

Two-fifths of the power that keeps civilized man going now comes from petroleum—in everyday speech, oil—or from the natural gas found with it under the earth. Total demand for power is growing too fast for oil to become less useful as atomic energy develops. In 1938 the world used 275 million tons of oil; today it uses over three times as much.

The U.S.A., producing a third of the world's output, yet has to import over a tenth of its needs; and each year it uses nearly a twelfth of its known reserves. Venezuela, the world's biggest exporter and second biggest producer, also keeps a wary eye on its reserves.

Western Europe (including Britain) has come to face the worst problems of all. Before 1939 it imported from the Americas two-thirds of the 40 million tons a year it then used. By 1959, lacking dollars, it depended on the Middle East for over three-quarters of its trebled imports. (It could produce only 12 million tons—one-tenth of its needs—from its own wells.)

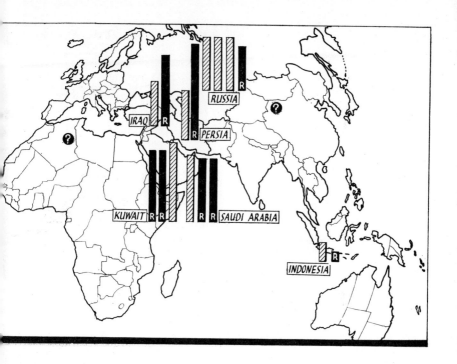

The Middle East oilfields' importance is long term as well as immediate (*41*). They contain two-thirds of all known reserves. The world's known reserves—today, 30,000 million tons—are continually increased by new discoveries (in the 1930s known reserves were no more than 3,000 million), and some experts think that as much as 140,000 million tons may be extracted before the earth runs dry. But the indications are that new discoveries will make the Persian Gulf area more, not less, important. Little is expected of the lesser producing countries (not marked), such as Rumania, Austria, France, Germany, British Borneo, Burma, India, Trinidad, Chile, Colombia, Argentina, and Egypt. Hopes of big new sources have been directed to the Sahara (*37*) and north-west China (*60*); and also to the tar sands near Lake Athabasca in Canada (*65*). The oil in these sands might double today's known reserves if it could be extracted cheaply. Vast shale deposits elsewhere in the Americas also present a tantalizing problem of extraction.

15

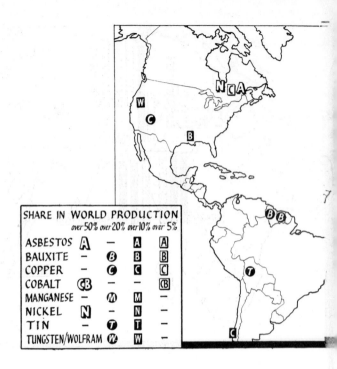

SHARE IN WORLD PRODUCTION			
	over 50%	over 20%	over 10%	over 5%
ASBESTOS	A	–	A	A
BAUXITE	–	B	B	B
COPPER	–	C	C	C
COBALT	CB	–	–	CB
MANGANESE	–	M	M	–
NICKEL	N	–	N	–
TIN	–	T	T	–
TUNGSTEN/WOLFRAM	W	W	–	–

4

SOME KEY MINERALS

Oil, coal, and iron are not the only natural resources that can give a country a special importance to the world. Rubber is another, as the second world war allies found when Japan seized Malaya, Siam, and the East Indies, which produce four-fifths of all natural rubber; only a huge increase in synthetic rubber production in North America saved the day. There are, too, a number of key minerals which, as the map shows, are concentrated in only a few areas to a degree that can sometimes have important political consequences.

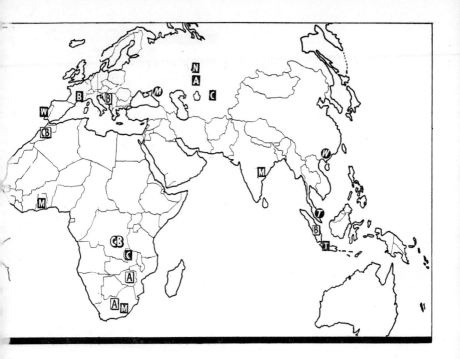

Thus, Bolivia, Malaya, and Indonesia produce two-thirds of the world's tin; British and Dutch Guiana, nearly half its bauxite (the main source of aluminium); Canada alone, two-thirds of its asbestos. Among the ferro-alloys, essential to the treating of steel for many purposes, Canada, again, yields over half of all nickel ore, the Belgian Congo nearly three-quarters of all cobalt; while Russia is by far the biggest source of manganese, and China of tungsten ore (wolfram).

5

ATOMIC GEOGRAPHY

The dawn of peaceful nuclear energy came not in 1945, when the first atom bomb was dropped (*14*), but in 1942, when Fermi proved it possible to control a chain reaction so that instead of an explosion it would produce intense heat—from which, in turn, electricity can be generated. 'Atomic electricity' has been produced in America, France, and Russia; and in October 1956, at Calder Hall in Cumberland, the world's first full-scale atomic power station began to feed electricity into Britain's national grid. The age of peaceful atomic power had finally arrived.

By 1975 Britain may be producing atomic power equivalent to 70 million tons of coal a year. And atomic power may soon be trans-

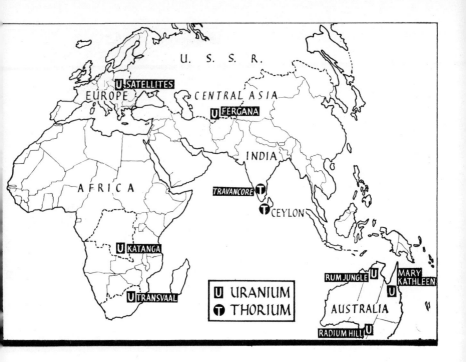

forming the outlook for countries that lack coal, oil, or hydro-electric power and for areas where industry cannot yet develop because of the high cost of hauling fuel there.

Despite the development of 'breeder reactors' in which nuclear fuel may be made to replace itself, and the prospect of ultimately finding a limitless source of energy in sea water, attention is still centred on places where there are rich and easily worked deposits of uranium ore, the main source of nuclear fuel, and of thorium, a secondary source. Canada may soon be producing 14,000 tons of uranium metal a year, America 12,000, and South Africa 5,000. Australia, Rhodesia, and the Belgian Congo are other major producers of uranium; in western Europe, France and Portugal contain sizeable deposits, and France produced 500 tons in 1958. Russia is probably obtaining about 8,000 tons a year from Central Asia, East Germany, Hungary, and other East European sources.

6

DOLLAR, POUND, AND ROUBLE

Since the second world war the great majority of countries have limited their imports from 'hard currency' areas, because they could not balance their trade with those areas in a free market. The United States and Canada are the biggest hard-currency countries, but the 'dollar area' as defined by Britain and others for the purpose of exchange control also includes several Latin American countries, the Philippines and Liberia. At the end of 1958, Britain and most of Western Europe were able to ease these controls, but they have still to achieve full 'convertibility', which means standing the strain of allowing a completely free exchange of currencies.

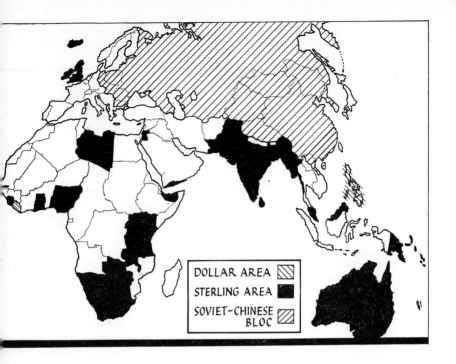

The sterling area is a close-knit currency group, which accounts for a quarter of the world's trade. Its members have their own separate currencies (e.g. India's rupee) and control their own payments, but the pound sterling is a common unit for payments between them, and most members contribute to, and draw from, a joint pool of dollars kept in London. The sterling 'scheduled territories' embrace the whole Commonwealth except Canada, plus the Irish Republic, Iceland, Libya, Jordan, and Burma.

The communist world has the tightest currency controls of all. Although there is a 'rouble area' in the sense that the currencies of the satellite countries, and to a lesser degree that of China, are linked to the Russian rouble, methods of payment between all these countries have been shrouded in secrecy, and they prefer to use dollars, sterling, gold, or other means for their trade with the outside world.

7

ONE WORLD?

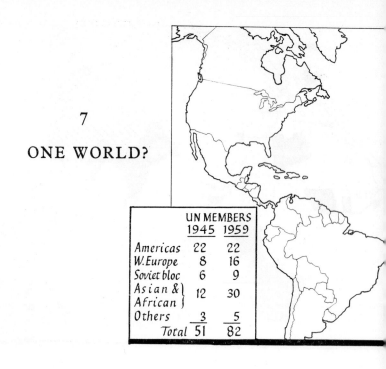

| | UN MEMBERS | |
	1945	1959
Americas	22	22
W. Europe	8	16
Soviet bloc	6	9
Asian & African	12	30
Others	3	5
Total	51	82

Interdependence is the hallmark of today's world. In our daily life we take for granted the flow of trade across continents and oceans. In the second world war, fighting ranged from the Arctic to the south Pacific, and since then the development of long-range nuclear missiles has made war a still more universal threat (*13*). Yet the world remains divided into over 80 sovereign states, each jealous of their independence; and their number is actually increasing as former dependencies become free.

The world's one-ness is recognized in the existence of many international organizations, the most important being the United Nations. Like its pre-war predecessor, the League of Nations, the UN, created in 1945, provides its member states (82 of them in 1959, against 51 original members) with means of settling disputes and working together—when they are willing. It has played a part in ending or limiting conflicts in Greece (*31*), Lebanon and Jordan (*45*), Persia (*46*), Kashmir (*48*), and Indonesia (*54*). It has watched over eleven Trust Territories, and decided the fate of Italy's former col-

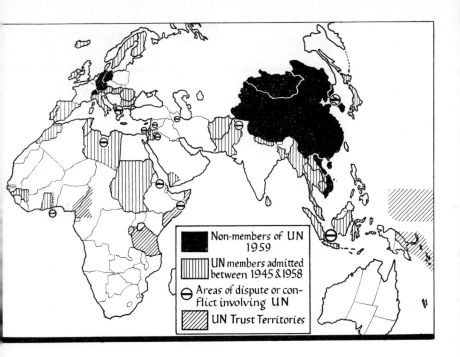

onies (*35*). Under its flag, soldiers from many countries have resisted aggression in Korea (*62*) and helped to restrict conflict in Palestine and Sinai (*40, 44*).

Yet it has been unable to solve many of the problems of a world which is in reality divided—a division reflected in the list of countries still unrepresented in the UN. Germany (*16*), Korea (*61*), and Vietnam (*52*) are themselves divided, a communist regime controlling part of each country. China is a member, but—mainly because its communist rulers fought against the UN in Korea—a majority of other members still regard the Nationalists on Formosa (*57*) as the lawful Chinese government. Mongolia, a Russian satellite state, has been refused admission. Switzerland feels that it can best maintain its tradition of neutrality by remaining outside the UN, although Swiss Geneva, formerly the seat of the League of Nations, is a centre of UN activities second only to the headquarters in New York.

8

DIVIDED
WORLD

Two great lines of division, one sharp, one blurred, cut across the world map. The sharp line is the 'iron curtain', the boundary of the communist system controlled from Moscow and Peking. In 1939 Russia was the only communist state, but after 1945 'satellite' communist rule was imposed in the parts of eastern Europe and of Korea occupied by the Russian army (*15*, *16*, *61*); in 1949 the communists won the Chinese civil war, and in 1954 a communist state was set up in North Vietnam (*52*). By then 13 communist governments existed, although one, in Jugoslavia, had thrown off Moscow's authority (*29*). The others—including Poland, which has won a degree of independence, and China, which is only indirectly dependent on Russia—form a bloc united in its declared aim of establishing communism throughout the world and in its policy of isolating its peoples from normal access to the outside world. Formally linked together by alliances, such as the 1955 Warsaw Pact and the 1950 Russian-Chinese alliance, the communist states are in reality bound by far stronger ties.

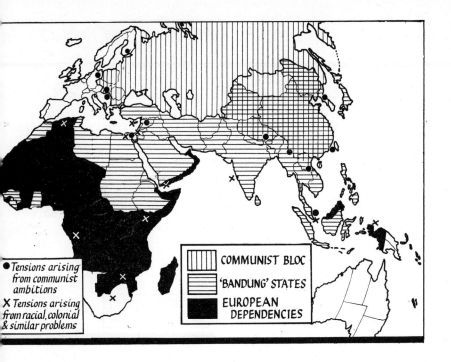

● Tensions arising
from communist
ambitions
X Tensions arising
from racial, colonial
& similar problems

		COMMUNIST BLOC
		'BANDUNG' STATES
		EUROPEAN DEPENDENCIES

The blurred line is primarily one of colour, with, on the one side, 'the West', the European–American–Australasian peoples; on the other, the 'Bandung' world of Asian and African peoples (*11*). Since 1939, some 700 million Asians and Africans have become independent of European rule (*9*); but suspicion and racial tension still arise wherever white dominance or privilege is regarded as out-lasting its day—whether in colonial forms, as in Goa (*50*) and New Guinea (*54*); in the shape of economic control, as in the Middle East oilfields (*41, 45*); or even in the form of western alliances with Asian states (*46, 55, 64*) and offers of economic aid to them (*12*). Conflict or tension is particularly likely where large white communities live alongside non-whites, as in parts of Africa (*32–34, 38*) and of the United States (*66*). Britain itself was shocked in 1958 by some violent, though very limited, attacks on West Indian and African immigrants. Resentment of colour prejudice and white privilege varies greatly, but it adds up to a formidable world force.

INDEPENDENCE
DUE IN 1960

9

FREEDOM WON AND LOST

The biggest change in the world map since the war of 1939–45 has been the appearance of 22 new sovereign nations, mostly in Asia and Africa, with a combined population of over 700 millions. Never before had so many colonies and other dependencies achieved freedom in so short a period. Japan and Italy lost their overseas possessions by defeat in the second world war (*35, 63*), while Denmark conceded independence to Iceland, and France to Syria and Lebanon. The post-war wave of emancipation was marred by large-scale fighting in some countries, particularly in Indonesia (*54*), Vietnam and the other states of Indo-China (*52*), and French North Africa (*38*).

26

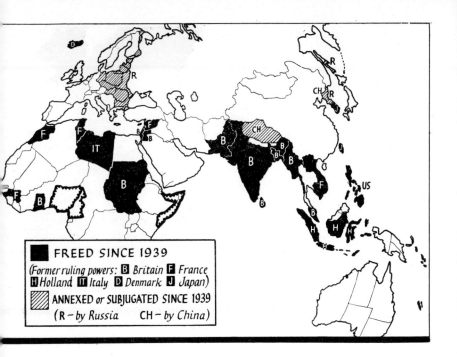

FREED SINCE 1939

(Former ruling powers: **B** Britain **F** France
H Holland **IT** Italy **D** Denmark **J** Japan)

ANNEXED or SUBJUGATED SINCE 1939
(R − by Russia   CH − by China)

But in India and Pakistan (*47*), the Philippines, Burma, Ceylon,
Sudan, and Ghana (*36*), Britain and America transferred power to
the new governments in an orderly and cooperative manner. Malaya
(*53*) obtained independence peacefully in 1957, and (French) Guinea
(*36, 37*) in 1958. And Nigeria (*36*), Cameroons (*36, 37*), Somalia
(*35*) and Cyprus (*31*) are due to become independent in 1960.

In contrast, the years since 1939 have also seen the two big
communist powers annexing large territories, extinguishing small
nations, and reducing others to the status of helpless 'satellites'.
Russia has directly annexed areas in Europe and the Far East with
25 million inhabitants, including the formerly sovereign Baltic
states, Estonia, Latvia, and Lithuania (*18*), and has subjugated six
other East European countries, comprising another 95 million people.
China has occupied Tibet, and in 1959 it had to suppress a national
revolt there (*60*); and Russia and China have jointly made themselves
masters of North Korea.

SOVEREIGN MEMBERS
OTHER SOVEREIGN STATES
formerly under British control
DEPENDENCIES NEAR
EMANCIPATION
OTHER DEPENDENCIES

10

EVOLVING COMMONWEALTH

In 1957 Ghana became the ninth and Malaya the tenth sovereign member of the Commonwealth, which has now become a unique association of fully independent states in all five continents. Half a dozen more British dependencies are also nearing full emancipation, including the West Indies and Nigeria (*68*, *36*). In Central Africa, statehood waits on assurance that the white population will give the Africans a fair deal (*33*). For Malta (*28*), the idea of integration with the United Kingdom, on somewhat the same basis as Northern Ireland (*27*) has been discussed, but in 1959 this no longer seemed acceptable.

Sovereign members of the Commonwealth are free to adopt a

28

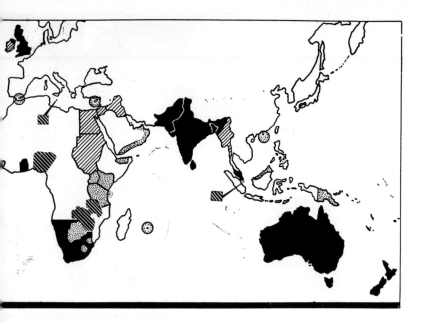

republican system (as India and Pakistan have done), or to leave the Commonwealth altogether (as Burma and the Irish Republic have done). They have no obligation to follow a common policy, and in fact are often at loggerheads on particular issues, such as the 1956 conflict in Egypt (*44*), Kashmir (*48*), and the rights of Indians and Pakistanis in South Africa (*32*). It is sometimes argued that so loose an association has no value. But the member countries themselves seem aware of its value, for they have held on to their membership despite their quarrels; while the Burmese have been known to express regret at their hasty decision to withdraw, and the Irish have retained links with Britain which give them many of the practical advantages of Commonwealth membership. For Egypt, the Sudan, Iraq, and Palestine, which were never technically regarded as British territories, the question of Commonwealth membership has not arisen.

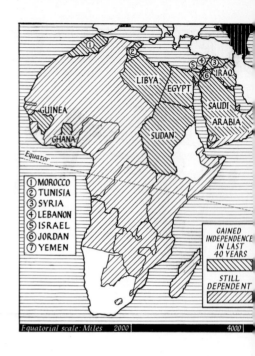

LIBYA
EGYPT
GUINEA
SAUDI
ARABIA
GHANA
SUDAN
IRAQ
Equator

① MOROCCO
② TUNISIA
③ SYRIA
④ LEBANON
⑤ ISRAEL
⑥ JORDAN
⑦ YEMEN

GAINED
INDEPENDENCE
IN LAST
40 YEARS

STILL
DEPENDENT

Equatorial scale: Miles   2000   4000

II

ASIA AND AFRICA

The conference which 29 Asian and African governments held at
Bandung, in Indonesia, in 1955 was a symbol of the great change
that had swept across their two continents. At the time of the first
world war there were only eight sovereign states in Asia and Africa,
and of these only Japan was a power to be seriously reckoned with;
almost everywhere else in the Asian–African world, including the
Arab domains of the crumbling Turkish Ottoman empire, West
European, American, or Russian rule or influence prevailed. The
Turkish collapse in 1918 allowed the Arabs to begin their movement
toward independence (39), but not until after the second world war
did the great retreat of the European (and Japanese) empires begin
—partly under the impact of war and of newly articulate nationalism,
partly because the ruling powers recognized that it was time to hand

over responsibility to peoples whom they had been training to handle their own affairs.

The Bandung meeting, which has given its name to the Afro-Asian group of nations, was a rallying point for a further assertion of national freedom. Communist China's star role at the conference revealed much difference of opinion between those Asians who feared the new strength of the communist powers, and those who, like India and Indonesia, saw no danger in it. It was easier for all to unite in urging the retreating West Europeans to retreat faster than to form a solid front against communist encroachment from the north. The 'Bandung' governments have shown similar inclinations in the UN Assembly, where they now occupy 30 out of 82 seats. Unanimous in supporting Egypt in the Suez-Sinai conflict (*44*), they were divided in their attitudes to Russia's onslaught on Hungary (*15*). At the end of 1958, the quickened tempo of the pressure for independence in Africa (*32*) was marked by a conference of nationalist parties at Accra, the capital of Ghana.

12

AID FOR
POORER
COUNTRIES

Since 1945 about £6,000 million ($17,000 mn.) worth of economic aid has been provided for the backward areas of Asia, Africa, Latin America, and the Mediterranean. The International Bank, often called the World Bank, has made loans totalling £650 million to these areas. Another United Nations project, the Technical Assistance Programme, has given them £70 million worth of expert service, equipment, and training. America has made much the biggest, Britain the second biggest, contribution to these UN activities.

Southern Asia also benefits from the Colombo Plan, launched in 1950 as a Commonwealth economic programme but later expanded to help all countries in the area. Australia, Britain, Canada, and New Zealand have provided about £300 million worth of equipment, funds, expert services, and training to the Asian participants in the plan—who also exchange experts and trainees among themselves, as do recipients of UN technical assistance.

Direct American economic aid for the 'underdeveloped' countries

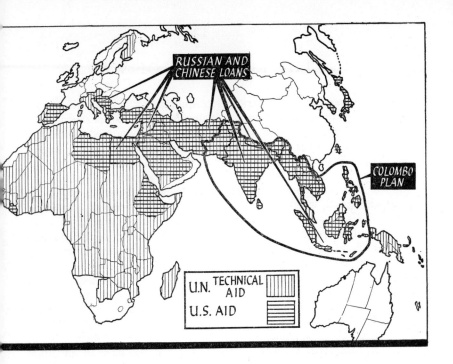

has overshadowed all these. America has provided them with some £4,500 million ($13,000 mn.) in grants, loans, and supplies. It has given aid not only to its allies but also to nearly all the 'uncommitted' Asian and Arab nations.

From 1954 onward Russia, which had previously denounced all aid programmes, even the UN ones, as 'imperialist plots', changed its tactics and began to offer loans to a chosen group of 'uncommitted' countries. In the next four years, Soviet (and Chinese) loans totalling £250 million were made to Afghanistan, Egypt, India, Indonesia, Jugoslavia, Nepal, and Syria. America alone provided £1,000 million in aid to 'uncommitted' nations in the same period, and they also obtained about £300 million through the World Bank, the Colombo Plan, and other schemes financed mainly by the western democracies. But Russia's loans, being something new, had a big propaganda effect at first. In 1958, however, the sudden withdrawal of Russian promises to Jugoslavia had a disillusioning effect.

THE LONG ARM OF WAR

In November 1958 America successfully tested an Atlas missile with a range of about 6,000 miles. It thus narrowed Russia's lead in the development of these weapons; Russia had announced a successful test of a similar inter-continental ballistic missile (ICBM) in August 1957. When the ICBMs are ready, there will be no major targets to which they could not carry their nuclear warheads.

The same applies to the nuclear-powered submarines now being developed, which will be able to cruise for long periods, submerged and invisible, off hostile coasts (and even under the Arctic ice—69), until ordered to fire their long-range missiles. America plans to have its first such submarine, equipped with Polaris missiles, in service by 1960; Russia's progress has not been revealed.

Meanwhile, to keep the deterrent in balance, radar stations along the Distant Early Warning (DEW) Line in northern Canada and Alaska keep watch for any Soviet 'surprise attack' across the Arctic, and America keeps a force of long-range bombers in constant readiness. Until the American ICBMs are ready, the intermediate-range missiles (IRBMs) which already exist will also have an important role in the 'deterrent'. With a range of about 1,500 miles, they cannot be fired from America to reach the communist powers' main strongholds (though Russia could, in contrast, use its own IRBMs against Europe, Japan, or the Middle East). Hence the installing of Thor IRBMs at bases in Britain and elsewhere in Europe in 1958 and 1959.

Hence, too, Russia's efforts to break up the western alliances and get American missiles and also American 'conventional' forces removed from both Europe and Asia. If all American forces went home, the communist powers, being stronger in conventional forces, might hope to get their way by a series of pressures and threats directed at smaller countries, estimating that America would always hesitate to invoke the perilous counter-threat of long-range retaliation. Russia has the advantage that it could withdraw its own forces from the 'satellite' states and still threaten western Europe from bases no farther away than Kaliningrad (formerly Königsberg).

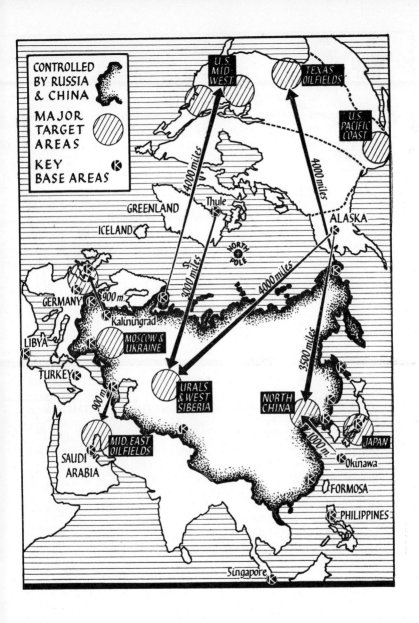

CONTROLLED BY RUSSIA & CHINA

MAJOR TARGET AREAS

KEY BASE AREAS

U.S. MID-WEST

TEXAS OILFIELDS

U.S. PACIFIC COAST

4000 miles

4000 miles

GREENLAND

Thule

ICELAND

NORTH POLE

ALASKA

3000 miles

4000 miles

GERMANY

900 m.

Kaliningrad

MOSCOW & UKRAINE

LIBYA

URALS & WEST SIBERIA

3500 miles

TURKEY

900 m.

MID. EAST OILFIELDS

SAUDI ARABIA

NORTH CHINA

1000 m.

JAPAN

Okinawa

FORMOSA

PHILIPPINES

Singapore

35

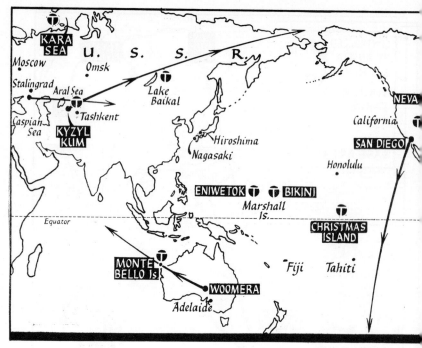

14

SPUTNIKS, ROCKETS, AND TESTS

In January 1959 Russia announced that it had fired a rocket past the
moon (220,000 miles from the earth). During 1958 American moon-
rockets had reached heights of 67,000 and 71,000 miles. These sallies
into space followed the success of Russia and America in shooting
artificial earth-satellites ('sputniks') into regular orbits round the
earth during 1957 and 1958. Circling at heights of up to 2,500 miles,
these satellites have transmitted important scientific information about
radiation and other conditions beyond the earth's atmosphere. But the
heavier of the satellites and the 'moon-probes' also had obvious military importance, for the rockets that carried them up were powerful
enough to carry inter-continental missiles with nuclear warheads (*13*).

America's first sputniks and long-range test rockets were fired
from Cape Canaveral; another launching base has been developed in
southern California. Russia has maintained secrecy about its launching bases, but the main one is reported to be in the Kyzyl Kum

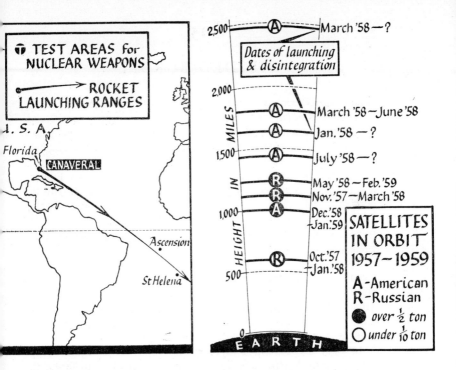

desert, south-east of the Aral Sea; its ICBM rockets have presumably been test-fired from there across northern Asia. Shorter-range Russian launching areas are thought to exist east of Stalingrad. British intermediate-range missiles have been test-fired from Woomera in South Australia along a range north-westward over the desert and the Indian Ocean.

The map also shows how empty expanses of land and sea have been used as sites for test explosions of nuclear weapons. (The only nuclear weapons used in war so far were used at Hiroshima and Nagasaki.) America has tested its hydrogen bombs in the area of the Marshall Islands in the Pacific (*64*), its less powerful nuclear weapons in Nevada and other Rocky Mountain states. Britain's hydrogen bomb tests have been at Christmas Island in mid-Pacific; and the British atom bomb has been tested near the Monte Bello Islands off the Australian coast. Russia, again, has kept its testing as secret as possible, but observations indicate that it has exploded hydrogen and atom bombs in Central Asia, farther east near Lake Baikal, and along its Arctic coast in the Kara Sea area.

37

DIVIDED EUROPE

When Nazi Germany's hold on Europe was broken in 1944–5, the advancing Russian army ensured communist control of Poland, Hungary, Rumania, and Bulgaria, and of parts of Germany and Austria. In Jugoslavia and Albania communist forces also triumphed, while Greece was saved only by swift British action. An 'iron curtain of silence' (in Sir Winston Churchill's words) fell across Europe, and the peoples east of it were cut off from normal contact with the outside world. There were two gaps in the 'curtain'—West Berlin, surrounded by communist territory but protected by western garrisons (*16*); and Czechoslovakia, whose democratic parties held out against strong pressure.

In 1948, however, the Czechoslovak communists, who had been steadily gaining control of the police and army, used this power to stage a *coup*, and transformed the country into a police state. In the same year the Jugoslav communists stopped taking Moscow's orders and, with western support, defied violent threats and pressures from Russia and its remaining satellites (*29*).

In 1955 the 'curtain' swayed again. Russia withdrew its troops from eastern Austria, and appealed to the Jugoslavs to forget the past. But its talk of 'relaxation', intended to beguile Germans and other westerners, had unexpected consequences in eastern Europe. In 1956 Moscow had to compromise with a Polish government which, while still led by communists, was under strong pressure from below to assert the nation's own interests. And in Hungary a nation-wide uprising, which was suppressed by the Russian army in defiance of repeated United Nations calls for a cease-fire, showed how intolerable the peoples of eastern Europe found their rulers, even after a decade of communist indoctrination. About 150,000 Hungarians were able to escape to the west in 1956 before the 'curtain' fell again.

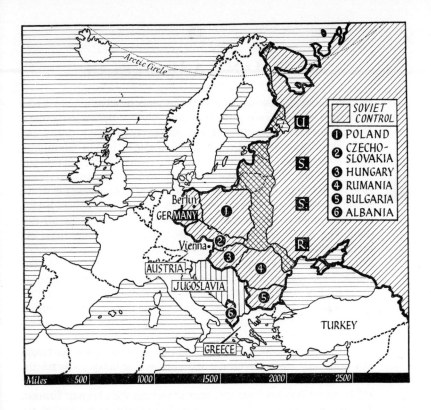

GERMANY AND BERLIN

In 1959 Russia's new demand that the western allies should with-draw from Berlin focused attention once more on post-war Europe's greatest territorial problem—the division of Germany that arose when the victorious western and Russian armies met in the middle of the country in 1945. Both Germany and Austria were then divided into four zones under the military administration of Russia, America, Britain, and France. Berlin and Vienna, which in each case fell with-in the Russian zone, were likewise divided into sectors controlled by the four powers. In Austria, a government recognized by all the occupying powers was set up and free elections held in 1945, al-though the Russians did not agree to a withdrawal until 1955 (23). But in Germany the Russians ignored their promises that the country should be treated as a unit, and rapidly turned their zone (black on the map) into a communist state. By 1948 the western allies had to give up hope of Russian cooperation and put through long overdue reforms in their zones alone. Russia then blockaded West Berlin, confident that this would make the West give ground; but a massive Anglo-American airlift supplied $2\frac{1}{2}$ million Berliners with food, coal, and other essentials for eleven months, and in May 1949 Russia lifted the blockade.

The western zones were then united to form the German Federal Republic with its capital at Bonn, while the Russians declared their zone a 'Democratic Republic'. In 1955 the western allies gave up their rights as occupying powers, although their forces remained in Western Germany by agreement. The Federal Republic, with 51 million inhabitants, has made a dramatic post-war recovery, while the Soviet zone's communist regime and relative poverty have driven three million Germans to flee westward, leaving it with a population of only $17\frac{1}{2}$ million.

Germans have become increasingly anxious to see their country reunited; but up to 1959 Russia insisted that any settlement must include a privileged position for its communist protégés, and the breaking up of the Atlantic alliance (19). There also remained the problem of Germany's new frontier with Poland (17). On the other hand, the Saar (22) had been reunited to Germany.

In November 1958 Russia announced that during 1959 it would

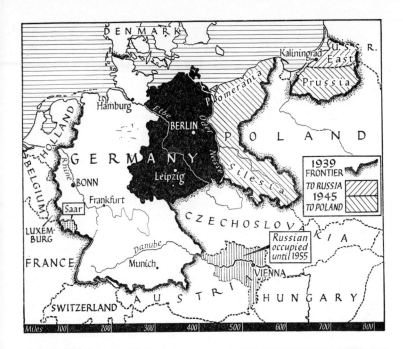

hand over to the east German communists its powers in regard to the
western allies' access to Berlin by
air, road and rail. Russia also
asked the allies to leave West Berlin
—which meant leaving its inhabitants in the power of the communist
'Democratic Republic'. The allies
refused, but anxiously discussed
what they should do if the communists again began to obstruct
their routes to isolated Berlin,
90 miles beyond the 'iron curtain'.

POLAND'S FRONTIERS

In 1939 Poland was partitioned between Germany and Russia after only twenty years of independence. At the end of the war Russia was in complete control of Poland, and in effect shifted the country bodily westwards. The half of Poland's pre-war territory which Russia had seized in 1939 was now ceded to Russia by treaty (*18*). On the other hand, some six million Germans were expelled from Silesia, Pomerania, southern East Prussia, and Danzig, and these areas were put under Polish control.

Poland thereby gained an extensive Baltic coastline and the coal and other industrial resources of Silesia, and got rid of its former restive minorities—Ukrainians, Byelorussians, and Lithuanians—in the east. But it was landed with the problem of the Germans' unwillingness to accept as final the new western frontier, the Oder–Neisse line, so called from the rivers along which it runs. Although many Poles, including some of those who had lost their homes in the east, were settled in the territory taken from Germany, much of the land became derelict; and while some German extremists talked of regaining all of it, among more moderate Germans there was hope of eventually negotiating a limited revision to enable some of the expelled Germans to return. Russia had agreed with the western allies that the final definition of this frontier must await a peace treaty with Germany, and because of the division of Germany there is still no peace treaty.

The Poles' anxiety about the Oder–Neisse line gives Russia a strong hold on them, and is partly responsible for the fact that in 1956, after winning a degree of independence from Russia, they did not try to follow Jugoslavia's example and make themselves fully independent. Another factor is that as long as East Germany remains under Russian occupation Poland is almost surrounded by Soviet forces, and its new government has had to agree to let the Red Army remain in Poland.

RUSSIA'S TERRITORIAL GAINS

During and after the second world war, Russia gained by treaty or outright annexation some 190,000 square miles of territory in Europe, with a population of over 24 million people.

In 1940, by agreement with Nazi Germany, Russia occupied the three Baltic countries, Estonia, Latvia, and Lithuania, which, like Finland, freed themselves from Russian rule after the 1917 revolution. Their political leaders and thousands of other 'dangerous' individuals were either killed or deported, and the three nations were absorbed into the Soviet Union, with the nominal status of member republics. Similar status was given to most of Bessarabia, which Russia took from Rumania after the war; but this new 'Moldavian Republic' was shut off from the sea by the incorporation in the Ukraine of the strip of coast running south to the Danube delta (30).

There was an ethnographic basis for Russia's action in taking from Poland and Czechoslovakia areas mainly populated by Ukrainians and Byelorussians. But in taking territory from Finland and Germany, Russia acted on purely strategic grounds. Finland's only Arctic port, Petsamo, was taken over; further south, a Finnish population of half a million was uprooted in order to push the frontier further away from Leningrad. In annexing the northern half of East Prussia, the Russians also had a strategic motive; the German population was removed and Russians brought in to secure the area around Königsberg, renamed Kaliningrad, and this area is administered as part of the Soviet Union's Russian member republic, although separated from it by the nominally autonomous Lithuanian and Byelorussian republics. Russia thereby strengthened its new hold on the Baltic coast (24), and on Poland.

The post-war acquisitions brought the Soviet frontier to within 150 miles of Warsaw, Bucharest, and Budapest. One effect of this was illustrated by the speed with which the Red Army could move in to crush the Hungarian revolt of 1956. Before the war, Russia had not even had a common frontier with Hungary.

1. FINLAND
2. ESTONIA
3. LATVIA
4. LITHUANIA
5. EAST PRUSSIA
6. POLAND
7. RUTHENIA
8. BUKOVINA
9. BESSARABIA

Petsamo

FINLAND

1938

Vyborg

Leningrad

Kaliningrad

Vilna

Brest-Litovsk

1938

Lwow

1938

GERMANY   POLAND

CZECHOSLOVAKIA

HUNGARY

RUMANIA

JUGOSLAVIA

BULGARIA

U S S R

SOVIET GAINS
SOVIET DOMINATED

Miles   500   1000   1500

45

19

ATLANTIC ALLIANCE

By 1947 there was growing alarm in western Europe, where post-war disarmament had been quick, over the continued presence of huge Russian forces in the heart of Europe, the creation of police states in eastern Europe and the building up there of 'satellite' armies under Soviet control. In March 1948, just after the communist *coup* in Czechoslovakia (*15*), a defensive alliance, the Brussels treaty, was signed by Britain, France, Holland, Belgium, and Luxemburg.

The Brussels allies, however, were clearly not strong enough to counter-balance Soviet and satellite armed strength and to free Europe from fear of being swamped by communism. They sought the support of the United States. Traditional American reluctance to get entangled in alliances was overcome after several menacing

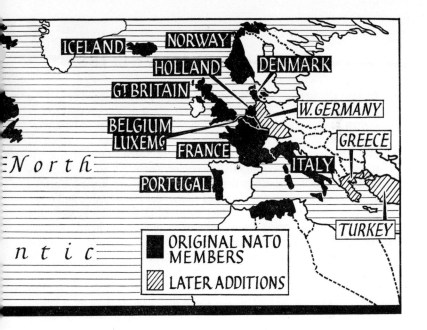

ICELAND NORWAY HOLLAND DENMARK GT.BRITAIN W.GERMANY BELGIUM LUXEMG FRANCE GREECE ITALY PORTUGAL TURKEY

North

ntic

■ ORIGINAL NATO MEMBERS

▨ LATER ADDITIONS

communist moves—the Czechoslovak *coup*, Soviet threats to Finland and Norway, and the Red Army's blockade of West Berlin (*16*). In April 1949 the United States and Canada joined with the five Brussels allies and with Italy, Norway, Denmark, Iceland, and Portugal in setting up the North Atlantic Treaty Organization. The twelve 'Nato' allies pledged joint resistance to any attack on one of them in Europe (overseas dependencies were excluded) or on their forces stationed in Germany or Austria.

The communist attack in Korea in 1950 (*62*) made the allies fear a 'European Korea', and they decided to give Nato more workable machinery for joint defence. A Supreme Headquarters, Allied Powers in Europe (Shape), was set up near Paris, with General Eisenhower as its first head, and an international command system was organized to take over in the event of war.

In 1952 Greece and Turkey joined the Atlantic alliance, and in 1955 Western Germany became Nato's fifteenth member (*20*).

WEST EUROPEAN UNITIES

In 1955 the five-member Brussels treaty (*19*) was enlarged to include Italy and Western Germany. The new seven-nation group became known as Western European Union (WEU). All its members were also allies in Nato, but the Union served the special purpose of providing safeguards against a revival of German aggressiveness without discriminating against Germany alone. All seven members agreed to limit the strength of their forces in continental Europe, and a control system was designed to see that these limits, and other pledges given in the Paris Agreements of October 1954, were not violated. Those agreements included a pledge by Britain not to reduce the effective strength of its forces on the mainland, unless four of the seven allies agreed or a grave emergency occurred overseas.

WEU is only one of the new bonds between West European countries. Since 1947 all the European democracies have been linked by the Organization for European Economic Cooperation (OEEC), which was formed to handle the European Recovery Programme (or 'Marshall Plan') but has outlasted it. Since 1949, all except Switzerland have sent ministers and members of parliament to the Council of Europe at Strasbourg. Smaller groups have formed closer bonds, e.g. the Scandinavians (*24*), and Belgium, the Netherlands, and Luxemburg, which have formed an economic union known as Benelux.

In 1951, France, Italy, Western Germany, and the Benelux trio created the European Coal and Steel Community (the 'Schuman Pool'). These six nations also tried to create a Defence Community (EDC) controlling a single European army, but this fell through in 1954, the Paris Agreements and WEU being devised as a substitute.

In 1958 the 'Six' set up an atomic energy community (Euratom) and a European Economic Community, generally described as a Common Market (*21*).

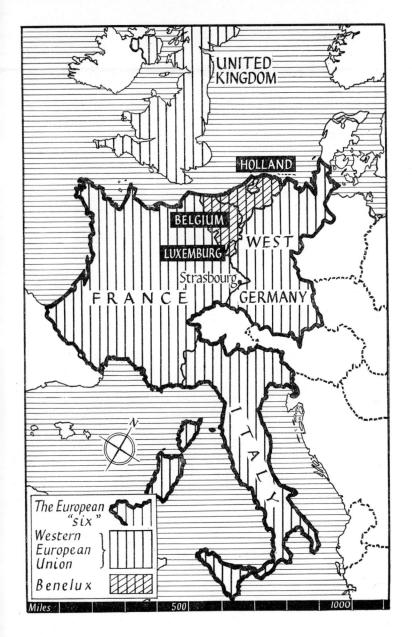

The European "six"

Western European Union }

Benelux

FREE TRADE IN EUROPE

At the beginning of 1959, the European 'Six' (20) made the first tariff cuts required by their agreement to create a Common Market. Their plan is to bring into being a customs union by progressively cutting down tariffs on trade with each other and adopting uniform tariffs for trade with other countries. They also want to enable their citizens to take jobs freely in any part of their Economic Community —a point of special interest to Italy; to make it easier for investment capital to flow between the six countries, and to launch other co-operative economic projects.

Britain was not prepared to join the Six in their Common Market, but in 1956, realizing that the creation of this market would favour continental competitors, the British government launched the idea of setting up a European Free Trade Area, associated with the Common Market but less far reaching in its effects. The basic idea was that countries in the Free Trade Area should progressively reduce tariffs between themselves and the Common Market, but could maintain separate tariffs for trade with other countries— which, for Britain, would make it easier to solve the problem of the existing Commonwealth trade preferences. The Scandinavian countries, Austria, and Switzerland were thought likely to follow Britain's example if she succeeded with the Free Trade Area plan.

The Common Market group has a population of over 160 million —comparable with America's or Russia's; and if the Free Trade Area members were added, the total would be 240 million. The economic advantages of free access to this huge market are evident.

But at the beginning of 1959 no agreement had been reached about the Free Trade Area, and the 'Six' were going ahead with the smaller Common Market by themselves.

COMMON MARKET ▤
FREE TRADE AREA ? ▨
OTHER O.E.E.C. MEMBERS ▧

Arctic Circle

NORWAY
Gt BRITAIN
SWEDEN
DENMARK
IRELAND
HOLLAND
W.GERMANY
BELG.M.
LUXEM.G.
FRANCE
AUSTRIA
SWITZ.P.
PORTUGAL
ITALY
GREECE
TURKEY

Miles   500   1000   1500   2000

THE SAAR

In 1945 the Saar border area was separated from Germany and linked with France by currency and customs unions. Political parties advocating reunion with Germany were banned. The French also obtained control of the Saar coal mines and steelworks. Their aim was not merely to obtain reparations for war losses but to offset the industrial strength of Germany's Ruhr. France, if it could count the Saar on its side, could keep roughly abreast of Germany in industrial power—while Germany, given the Saar, would leave France far behind.

However, the million Saarlanders speak and feel German. In 1935 they had voted themselves back into Germany after 15 years under League of Nations supervision. They took their second separation in 1945 quietly, but nationalist feeling revived as post-war Germany recovered. In 1952 it was proposed to 'Europeanize' the Saar as a part of the plans then being discussed for a European union. Although these plans fell through, France and Germany agreed in 1954 to try to Europeanize the Saar under a special statute. But in 1955 the Saarlanders rejected the statute in a referendum. Full political freedom was then restored, and parties eager for reunion with Germany came into power in the Saar. Fresh Franco-German negotiations followed, in which France relaxed its hold on Saar industries, while Germany agreed to the canalizing of the Moselle river so that Lorraine iron ore could be shipped out more cheaply. In January 1957 the Saar was politically reunited with Germany; and it was agreed that it should be economically integrated into Germany during 1959.

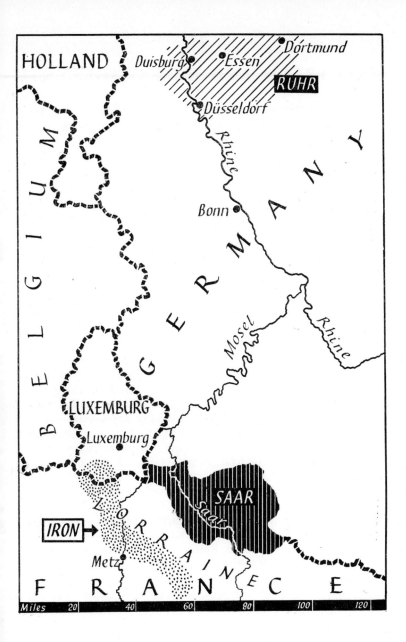

HOLLAND

Duisburg •Essen •Dortmund

RUHR

Düsseldorf

Rhine

BELGIUM

GERMANY

Bonn•

Mosel

Rhine

LUXEMBURG

Luxemburg•

IRON→

LORRAINE

SAAR

Saar

Metz•

FRANCE

Miles   20   40   60   80   100   120

23

'NEUTRALS' AND 'DISENGAGEMENT'

Between the Soviet bloc and the Atlantic allies lie five 'neutral' countries. The origins of their neutrality differ. Jugoslavia is a communist state which, after successfully defying Russia (*15*, *29*), sought links with 'uncommitted' Asian and African countries such as India and Egypt rather than with other European 'neutrals'. Switzerland and Sweden are as democratic as their western neighbours, but have long traditions of non-involvement. The world has come to expect them to provide mediators and other impartial persons to help alleviate international conflicts; the present Secretary-General of the United Nations is Swedish, the International Committee of the Red Cross is Swiss, and Swiss Geneva is a favourite site for international conferences. Sweden's position is also partly a result of Finland's (*24*).

Finland and Austria are also democracies, but their neutrality is not traditional. It is part of the price each has paid to get Russia to leave it alone. After 1955, when the Russians withdrew from Austria on condition that it remained neutral, they sought to get other western countries to follow the 'Austrian example'. Their main aim was to get Germany neutralized on their terms, which included the winding up of the Atlantic allies' defence system. There have sometimes been hopes that Russia might let the East European countries as well as Germany become independent and neutral—which might make it less risky for the West to withdraw from Germany. Western discussion about 'disengagement' has envisaged withdrawal of all foreign forces from Germany, Poland, Czechoslovakia, and Hungary; the nearest communist offer up to 1959 was the 'Rapacki Plan' for removal of atomic weapons from Central Europe, with limited cuts in other arms. But in 1956, when Hungary appealed to be allowed to become neutral like Austria, the Russian army overthrew the Hungarian government and installed another obedient puppet regime. By this action, Russia also jeopardized its own effort to woo Jugoslavia back into the Soviet camp.

SWEDEN

FINLAND

GERMANY

Poland

Czechoslovakia

SWITZ⁴ AUSTRIA

Geneva

Hungary

JUGOSLAVIA

Miles 200   400   600   800   1000   1200

55

24

SCANDINAVIA AND RUSSIA

Traditional Scandinavian neutrality was shattered by Russia's attack on Finland in 1939 and Nazi Germany's occupation of Denmark and Norway in 1940. The Finns, hoping to regain the territory Russia had seized, joined the Germans in attacking it in 1941. Only Sweden remained neutral. But after 1945 the Scandinavians tried to restore their old ties. They set up, for example, a Nordic Council for regular consultation between ministers and members of their parliaments. A Scandinavian defence union was also discussed; but Denmark, Norway, and Iceland, fearing that this would not give them enough security, joined the Atlantic alliance in 1949.

Post-war Scandinavian fears arose largely from Russia's seizure of Estonia, Latvia, Lithuania, and half East Prussia, its occupation of East Germany and its grip on Poland (*15*, *18*). The south-eastern shores of the Baltic were thus all in communist hands. In the far north Russia, by annexing Finland's Arctic port, Petsamo (Pechenga), had reached the Norwegian border. Even the Swedes built up their defences, although they held to their 'alliance-free' policy—partly out of fear that, if they joined the western alliance, Russia would take retaliatory steps against Finland. The Finns had already lost to Russia an eighth of their country. In 1956 Russia handed back Porkkala, the base near Helsinki which it had occupied since 1945. But it kept a tight economic grip on Finland, and at the beginning of 1959 it was trying to use this to force the Finns to accept communists in their government.

25

DISPUTED WATERS IN THE NORTH

In 1960 a world conference will make another attempt to solve the problem of how much territorial water each nation may claim round its coasts. The Geneva conference in 1958 found no solution, and in 1959 the post-war trend to bigger claims was continuing (see also *54*). The sharpest dispute was between Britain and Iceland; Britain was using naval patrols to protect its fishermen off the Iceland coast from gunboats trying to enforce Iceland's new claim to a twelve-mile limit.

Until recently a majority of countries, including Britain, claimed only three miles of water. Norway and Iceland, whose coasts are among Europe's richest fishing grounds, claimed four and defined their four-mile limits by drawing a straight line across the mouths of bays and inlets, which, as their coasts are very irregular, enables them to bar large areas of sea to foreign fishermen. Britain and Norway took their dispute on this point to the International Court at The Hague. In 1951 the Court ruled that Norway's claim, being based on long tradition, was not a breach of international law (which is far from clear on the subject). In 1952 Iceland enforced a four-mile limit. The British trawler owners then secured a boycott of fish caught by the Icelanders themselves. Iceland, having lost the best customer for its biggest export, soon found a new one in Russia. By 1955 it was doing a quarter of all its trade with Russia and Russia's satellites.

This quarrel affected Iceland's attitude to the Atlantic alliance (*19*). It had joined Nato in 1949, but declined to have any foreign forces on its soil in peacetime (it has no forces of its own). In 1951, however, after the Korean war started, Iceland let America reactivate the air base near Reykjavik which it had built in 1941. Later, as the danger of war seemed to recede, and Iceland's quarrel with Britain and new links with Russia took effect, the 150,000 Icelanders changed their minds again, and in 1956 their parliament demanded that the Americans should withdraw. Negotiations on a withdrawal began, but after Russia's suppression of the Hungarian revolt (*15*), the Icelanders' attitude was somewhat moderated. At the end of 1956 a temporary settlement of the fishery dispute was reached. But in 1957 the people of the Danish Faeroe Islands in turn began to demand an extension of territorial waters.

In September 1958, Iceland extended its claim to twelve miles (which Russia also claims). Britain refused to recognize this new claim, and sent its naval patrols to ensure freedom to fish in certain sea areas between the four- and twelve-mile lines.

26

THE DUTCH BEAT BACK THE SEA

Europe's familiar coastline is being changed by the Dutch, who have a long tradition of gaining land from the North Sea in the form of low-lying 'polders' protected by dykes. Since 1919 they have been working on their most ambitious plan yet, a 60-year programme to win from the sea over half a million acres, which will enlarge their densely populated country by 7 per cent. The gulf formerly known as the Zuider Zee, now renamed the Ijsselmeer, was sealed off by a dam in 1932 and is slowly becoming a freshwater lake. Two big sections of it, the Wieringermeer (W) and North-East (NE) polders, have already been dyked, drained, and converted into farmland. In 1956 the dyke round a third polder, Eastern Flevoland (EF), was finished. By 1980 two more, Southern Flevoland (SF) and Markerwaard (M) will be reclaimed, and the twelfth province of the Netherlands will have risen from the sea. Its capital, Lelystad, has already been founded in the middle of the gulf.

Further south, the 'Delta plan' was launched in 1956 to dam the mouths of the Rhine and create another big freshwater lake. The Delta dams are designed to protect the south-east from storms like that of 1953, which flooded 375,000 acres and threatened the livelihood of four million people. They will also link the Zeeland islands with the mainland. Ultimately, the Dutch hope to build a continuous sea defence line extending to the Friesian islands in the north.

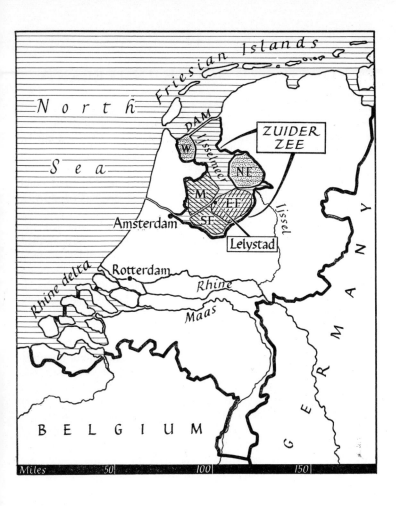

North Sea

Friesian Islands

DAM

IJsselmeer

ZUIDER ZEE

W

NE

M

EE

SE

Amsterdam

Lelystad

IJssel

GERMANY

Rhine delta

Rotterdam

Rhine

Maas

BELGIUM

Miles 50 100 150

27

NORTH AND SOUTH IN IRELAND

In 1958 the Irish Republic rounded up and placed in detention a number of suspected leaders of armed gangs. Since 1954 there has been a series of armed raids into Northern Ireland, carried out by secret societies such as the IRA ('Irish Republican Army'—not to be confused with the Irish Republic's army). The raids' chief object was to stir up feeling against the partition of Ireland; but their chief effect was to anger the Protestant Ulstermen of the north and make the division between north and south sharper.

The Republic was formally constituted as such, and left the British Commonwealth, in 1949. In fact, the territory, earlier called the Irish Free State, then Eire, had long been independent, having shed the ties with Britain retained in the 1921 treaty which ended five years of rebellion and repression. Its political leaders, while all pledged to the ending of partition some day, all disown and deplore the border raids and the whole idea of using force against the Ulstermen.

Northern Ireland (population 1·4 million, to the Republic's 2·9) chose in 1920 to remain a part of the United Kingdom, but obtained a system of home rule. In its own parliament at Belfast, a dozen out of a total of 52 seats are usually held by 'anti-partition' members, while two or three of the twelve M.P.s it elects to sit in London often take the same line. The total vote for anti-partition candidates has ranged between 120,000 and 170,000 in recent elections, out of an electorate of 900,000. While the Protestant religion and attachment to Britain and the British monarchy are enough to account for most Ulstermen's refusal to be ruled from Roman Catholic Dublin, another factor is the north's relative prosperity, which it owes largely to its membership of the United Kingdom. Southern Irishmen have flocked north, as well as to England and Scotland, to get better pay and social services.

It is sometimes argued (though no Dublin government has demanded it) that Fermanagh and Tyrone, where anti-partition M.P.s are usually elected, should be transferred to the Republic. Against this, however, it is argued that almost as many people would thereby be transferred against their will as those who might welcome the transfer. In both the constituencies concerned, anti-partition candidates have won by only very small majorities in recent elections.

NORTHERN IRELAND

IRISH

DUBLIN

REPUBLIC

Glasgow
SCOTLAND

BELFAST

Liverpool

WALES

1 LONDONDERRY 2 TYRONE
3 FERMANAGH 4 ARMAGH
5 DOWN 6 ANTRIM

Miles 100 200 300

28

GIBRALTAR AND MALTA

Although traditionally linked as Britain's two naval bases in the Mediterranean, Gibraltar and Malta today present different problems. Gibraltar, which Spain ceded to Britain in 1713 in exchange for Florida, is a tiny promontory, four miles long and less than a mile wide. Its 23,000 inhabitants (of mixed Italian, Moroccan, Jewish, British, and other origin) depend for their livelihood on the port and garrison, as do some 12,000 Spaniards who daily come in to work. Spain has long and sometimes loudly demanded Gibraltar, and in 1954 it began to apply some mild economic pressures, such as a ban on Spaniards making shopping visits to the colony.

The 320,000 Maltese inhabit two stony little islands, Malta and Gozo (together, 120 sq. miles). Their ancestors, after being ruled by the international order of Knights of St John since 1530, sought and obtained British protection in 1800. Their own language, somewhat resembling Arabic, was long scorned by the upper class, who preferred Italian. In the 1930s Fascist Italy, eager to oust Britain from the Mediterranean, wooed the Maltese but won over only a small minority. In the 1939–45 war most Maltese sided wholeheartedly with Britain, and endured bombing and privation with a courage honoured by the collective award of the George Cross. Post-war Italy makes no claim to the islands. After winning the 1955 elections, Mr Dom Mintoff's Labour Party sought 'integration' with Britain—meaning that Malta, while retaining home rule, would have parliamentary seats in London and social services approaching British levels. But in a referendum in 1956 less than half the electorate supported their Prime Minister, many voters being influenced by the conservative Catholic priesthood; and in 1958 Mr Mintoff resigned, having failed to get the financial terms he had sought from Britain. At the beginning of 1959 he was demanding complete independence; but without the British base and British aid Malta would be desperately poor.

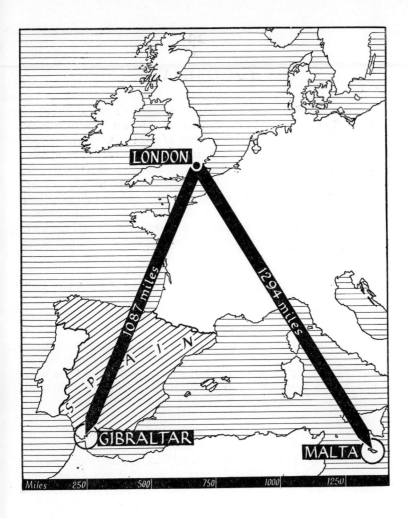

29

JUGOSLAVIA

Communism was imposed in post-war Jugoslavia not, as elsewhere in eastern Europe, by the Russian army, but by Tito's guerrilla army, which drove the German forces out of most of this mountainous country with help from the western allies. From 1945 to 1948, however, Jugoslavia was a loyal follower of Russia. It also had its own quarrel with the West, over Trieste, which it tried to seize in 1945. In the 1947 peace treaty with Italy, Jugoslavia secured the peninsula south of Trieste and the area north of it to the Austrian frontier (mainly populated by Slavs), but the western allies would not let it take Trieste itself, an essentially Italian city. Trieste remained under military administration, with an Anglo-American garrison in Zone A, including the city proper, and Jugoslav control of Zone B, until 1954, when Jugoslavia finally agreed to let Italy have Zone A and itself absorbed Zone B.

Meanwhile Jugoslavia had thrown off Russian domination in 1948 and survived six years of economic and political pressure from all the other communist countries. Its quarrel with Moscow left Albania out on a limb. Jugoslavia had helped the Albanian communists to establish themselves in power; but after 1948 Albania sided with Russia and, protected by its mountains, became a geographical curiosity—a Soviet satellite detached from the Soviet block.

Tito's rift with Russia disrupted the support which Jugoslavia, Albania, and Bulgaria had been giving to communist guerrillas in northern Greece, and Greece then soon succeeded in putting down the rebellion. Jugoslavia's relations with its non-communist neighbours slowly improved; and in 1953 it concluded with Greece and Turkey a treaty known as the Balkan Pact, which in 1954 was turned into a defensive alliance (*31*). Russia denounced the alliance as 'aggressive', but within a month had veered sharply round and was beginning to attempt a reconciliation with Jugoslavia.

This reconciliation did not survive the Hungarian revolt in 1956, which the Soviet rulers attributed largely to Tito's example of successful independence. By 1958 the other communist states were cutting down trade and denouncing Jugoslavia's 'revisionism', and Russia had cancelled its promises of economic aid (*12*).

AUSTRIA   HUNGARY

SOVIET
BLOC

ITALY

Zagreb

Trieste

Danube

RUMANIA

Sava

BELGRADE

J U G O S L A V I A

Split

BULGARIA

TRIESTE · 1945 — 54

ITALY

ANGLO-AMERICAN
ADMINISTRATION

A

TRIESTE

JUGOSLAVIA

ALBANIA

Tirana

B

JUGOSLAV
ADMINISTRATION

Salonika

EPIRUS

GREECE

MILES   10   20   30
Miles   100   200   300   400   500

30

THE DANUBE

Eight countries share the 1,700-mile Danube river, and its value as eastern Europe's biggest natural trade route has been sharply affected by political quarrels. In 1945 almost its whole length, from the Soviet-occupied zone of Austria down to the Black Sea, passed into the hands of Russia and its satellites. The trade that formerly flowed downstream from Austria and Germany was blocked. Russia, having annexed from Rumania an area stretching southward to the Danube mouth, insisted that the pre-war regulation of the river by a European commission must be revised, and formed a new Danube commission dominated by the communist states. Then came Jugoslavia's quarrel with Russia in 1948, and river traffic was further dislocated. While

the Russians, Rumanians, and Bulgars could bar Jugoslav access to the Black Sea, the Jugoslavs in turn could stop traffic between those three countries and the other satellites, Hungary and Czechoslovakia, which lay upstream.

When, six years later, Russia sought a reconciliation with Jugoslavia, Danube trade at last began to recover. The Jugoslavs and Rumanians embarked on a joint plan to improve the river channel along their border and to exploit it for hydro-electric power. In 1957 there was further progress when Austria completed a set of agreements with the communist states which gave its shipping the right to use the whole river down to the Black Sea.

Rumania had begun after the war to dig a canal from Constanza to the Danube, to eliminate the river's big northward bend near its mouth; but in 1953 the communist economy ran into such difficulties that work on this Black Sea canal was stopped.

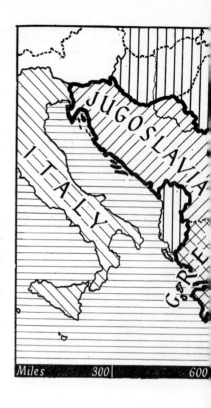

31

CYPRUS
AND THE
BALKAN
ALLIES

Almost as soon as Jugoslavia had linked itself with Greece and Turkey, two members of Nato, in the Balkan Alliance of 1954 (*29*), it began to receive conciliatory approaches from Russia which made it increasingly non-committal about the military aspects of the alliance. But the outlook for the new Balkan partnership was soon darkened by a more pressing problem, that of Cyprus.

Britain occupied Cyprus in 1878 by agreement with Turkey, and annexed it in 1914. Of its 500,000 inhabitants, four-fifths are of Greek and nearly a fifth of Turkish origin. Agitation among the Greek Cypriots for union with Greece (enosis) developed in the 1930s, and they regularly rejected British offers of limited self-government. In 1954 matters came to a head. Greece suggested negotiations on Cyprus. Britain refused, and—with the impending evacuation of its Suez Canal base in mind (*43*)—declared that it must

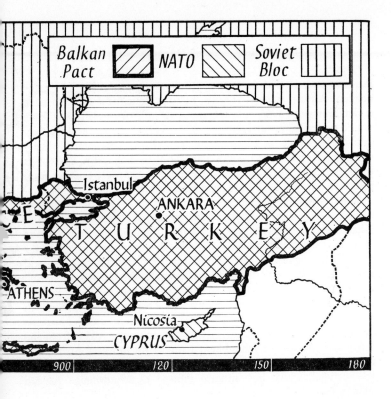

retain Cyprus as a strategic base for the defence of the Near and Middle East. Mounting unrest among the Greek Cypriots, encouraged by violent propaganda from Athens, was soon supplemented by murders and organized guerrilla attacks. An Anglo-Greek-Turkish conference in 1955 produced no solution, and was followed by an outbreak of anti-Greek violence in Turkey, where a campaign was launched for the partitioning of Cyprus.

In February 1959 Britain, Greece and Turkey reached an agreement, which was also accepted by the Greek Cypriots' leader, Archbishop Makarios. Cyprus was to become a republic, its independence internationally guaranteed, in 1960. Britain would keep its air base, and the republic's constitution would protect the position of the Turkish minority.

32

AFRICAN ACCELERATION

By 1960 over half of Africa's 225 million people will live in independent African states—whereas, in 1955, four-fifths of them were under European rule. The greater part of Africa will thus have passed under European control and re-emerged in one life-span, for, until the 'scramble for Africa' in the 1880s, Europeans controlled only the extreme north and south and some coastal strips elsewhere; tropical Africa was a mass of independent societies, ranging from primitive tribes to well organized feudal states.

With the attaining of independence by Libya (1951), Sudan (1955), Morocco and Tunisia (1956)—predominantly Arab countries—by Ghana (1957), Guinea (1958), Nigeria, Cameroons, and Somalia (due in 1960), and possibly French Togoland and others, over 75 million people will have passed out of European tutelage, and among the remaining 100 millions demands for independence will undoubtedly continue to spread. Even in the hitherto quiet Belgian Congo, African nationalism showed its first violent symptoms in 1959, and Belgium hastily promised political reforms. Thus the Congo will no longer shield eastern and southern Africa from the infectious example of triumphant nationalism in West Africa, and change may come sooner than expected even in the territories ruled by Portugal, which has hitherto refused to acknowledge African nationalism.

Changes can be expected in Africa's familiar boundaries, for many of these are artificial results of the 'scramble', which divided some tribes into two or three parts, and elsewhere lumped together peoples who have little in common. Some African nationalist leaders, fearing a breaking-up into small tribal states, are trying to create new federations (*36, 37*). But poor communications, and long distances between centres of population, make for disunity. And the Moslem religion (Islam) divides some Africans from others both in the west and along the east coast—while the Moslem Arab states along the north coast (*39*) are separated from tropical Africa by many things, including the Sahara desert.

But politics are most complex, and tensions sharpest, in areas settled by Europeans (*33, 34, 38*). Most of them, accustomed to a privileged status, cannot face the prospect of being dominated by the more numerous Africans—particularly when they are farmers who

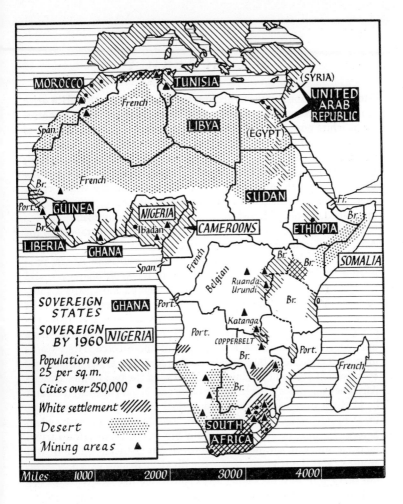

SOVEREIGN STATES GHANA
SOVEREIGN BY 1960 NIGERIA
Population over 25 per sq. m.
Cities over 250,000
White settlement
Desert
Mining areas

have sunk their capital in buying and developing land, and cannot, like engineers or doctors, seek new posts elsewhere if the Africans among whom they live advance to a dominant position.

33

SOUTH AFRICA

Most international issues affecting the Union of South Africa arise from the government's avowed aim of ensuring permanent control by its white population of three million (over half of them Afrikaners of Dutch origin, the rest mainly of British origin). The whites are outnumbered by the $9\frac{1}{2}$ million Africans, $1\frac{1}{4}$ million 'Coloureds', mostly of mixed race, and 400,000 Indians, but they have a monopoly of political power; and this is the only country where racial segregation (apartheid) and discrimination are being systematically intensified, a policy almost universally condemned abroad.

Proposals to solve the problem by carving out a separate state for Africans ('Bantustan') have foundered because the Union's economy is based on African labour. It is the richest country in Africa, producing half the world's gold and much of its wool, diamonds, and uranium (5); and although Africans are denied most skilled jobs, their earnings in its mines and factories are high enough to bring in a flow of labour from nearby territories, including the British protectorates of Bechuanaland, Basutoland, and Swaziland. South Africa has repeatedly demanded the transfer of these three 'High Commission Territories', but Britain has replied that under the Act of 1909 (which created the Union by federating the two former Dutch-Afrikaner republics with Britain's Cape and Natal colonies) it cannot hand them over without consulting their African inhabitants. The three protectorates' delicate position was illustrated in 1950, when Seretse Khama, heir to the chieftainship of the Bamangwato tribe, married an Englishwoman. White South African opinion was aroused, and the tribe itself sharply divided. Britain exiled Seretse, but in 1956 he and his family were allowed to live in Bechuanaland as private persons.

Some Afrikaners want to make South Africa a republic and to leave the Commonwealth; this has provoked talk of secession in Natal, where the whites are predominantly British. In 1955 Britain's naval base at Simonstown was transferred to the Union, which agreed, however, that Britain might use it in wartime.

South Africa has been repeatedly arraigned at United Nations meetings; by India and Pakistan for its treatment of its Indian population (mainly settled in Natal); by many countries for its general

racial policies, and for its refusal to place South-West Africa, which it formerly held as a League of Nations mandate, under UN trusteeship. The government regards the mandate as ended, and since 1950 South-West Africa has been represented in the Union parliament.

34

CENTRAL AND EAST AFRICA

In 1960 the Central African Federation set up in 1953 is to be reviewed and its future decided. The Federation unites two British protectorates, Nyasaland and Northern Rhodesia, and the virtually self-governing British colony of Southern Rhodesia. Each of these upland, landlocked areas has an African population of over 2 million, but whereas Southern Rhodesia has nearly 200,000 white settlers, the North has only 70,000 whites—largely concerned with the mines of the 'Copperbelt'—and Nyasaland only 7,000. The case for federating them was partly economic—Nyasa labour flows to the Copperbelt, the Kariba dam will by 1960 supply power both north and south of the Zambezi, and union could encourage investment; partly political—it was hoped that the Federation could in time become a sovereign and self-supporting state, based on 'partnership' between races. But by 1959 African fears of permanent domination by the white settlers, despite the present constitutional safeguards, had grown, and in Nyasaland a campaign to break up the Federation was under way. In February 1959 many African nationalist leaders were arrested on suspicion of planning a violent outbreak, and emergency rule was imposed against a background of local riots and uneasiness.

Central African federation in 1953 helped to set off a crisis in Uganda (population $5\frac{1}{2}$ million Africans, 55,000 Indians, 8,000 whites). Its most advanced tribe, the Baganda, a million strong, who have a long-established monarchical state, Buganda, feared absorption into a British East African federation dominated by Kenya, and demanded independence for Buganda alone. Their ruler, the Kabaka, refused to accept some proposed reforms, and Britain exiled him from 1953 to 1955. In Uganda, aversion persists to any idea of union with Kenya, for in Kenya 60,000 whites and 200,000 Indians and Arabs dominate the economy and have more political powers than the 6 million Africans.

In Kenya itself, among the Kikuyu, the tribe most affected by the settlers' occupation of the 'White Highlands', north of Nairobi, the terrorist Mau Mau movement broke out in 1952 and was not fully mastered until 1955. Kenya Africans are now pressing their demands by regular political means, but there is still some tendency to revert to atavistic secret societies.

In 1958 nationalism emerged strongly in the first general elections

held in Tanganyika, a British trust territory ($8\frac{1}{2}$ million Africans, 20,000 whites, 90,000 Indians and Arabs). And in Zanzibar, a protectorate with a Moslem sultan (population 280,000, including 60,000 Arabs and Indians), Arab leadership seems to be yielding ground to African nationalism.

35

ETHIOPIA AND THE SOMALIS

As 1960, Somalia's deadline for independence, approaches, the 'Horn' of Africa faces problems which affect Ethiopia and Kenya as well as the three Somali territories.

Until Fascist Italy conquered it in 1936, Ethiopia (Abyssinia) was the only sovereign state in eastern Africa, ringed round by European dependencies. During the second world war British Commonwealth forces freed it and restored the Emperor Haile Selassie to his throne. They also subdued the two Italian coastal colonies, Eritrea and Somalia. In 1950 the United Nations Assembly approved the federation of Eritrea with Ethiopia, which thus acquired a sea coast, although its most direct outlet remains the railway to French Djibuti. Somalia's fate was different; the Assembly decided that Italy should administer it as a UN Trust Territory until 1960.

The 3 million Somalis—Moslem nomads, under strong Arab influence—have been divided between the British, Italian and French Somalilands, eastern Ethiopia and north-east Kenya. Somali nationalists are campaigning for the union of all these areas as soon as possible after 1960. But French Somaliland voted in 1958 to remain linked with France (37); in the British protectorate political development has been relatively slow; and Ethiopia shows no wish to hand over the Somali-populated Ogaden area.

Up to 1959, a long-standing dispute over the line of the Ethiopia–Somalia frontier had not been settled, despite lengthy discussions in UN meetings and elsewhere. And since the war, Ethiopia has also insisted that Britain should fulfil an agreement made in 1897 to hand over the Haud and Reserved areas, border pasturelands which the protectorate tribes claim to be essential for the grazing of their herds and flocks. Ethiopian troops entered these areas in 1955 and, in violation of the agreement with Britain, began to force the nomad tribesmen to surrender their British passports and accept Ethiopian nationality. Ethiopia's actions aroused bitter resentment among the protectorate tribes, who have unsuccessfully urged Britain to appeal to the United Nations on their behalf.

36

WEST AFRICA

By 1960 there will be at least five sovereign states in West Africa—old-established Liberia, Ghana, Guinea (37), Nigeria, and Cameroons; and possibly others too.

Post-war political advance in all four British West African dependencies, where no white settlement complicates the scene, had led the Gold Coast, now renamed Ghana, to full sovereignty by 1957. British Togoland joined Ghana after a plebiscite, being thus the first United Nations trust territory to end its trustee status.

Nigeria is to become a sovereign state in 1960. With 35 million people (to Ghana's 5 million) it is Britain's biggest dependency. But it has met with some difficulty in moving towards full independence on a federal, three-region, basis. In Ghana the Ashanti and the northern tribes, although fearing domination by the more numerous

80

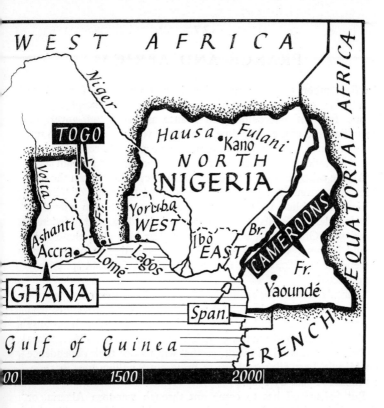

and politically active southerners, accepted a unitary constitution in 1957. But in Nigeria there are not only similar fears in the Moslem north, which contains half the population, but also rivalries between south-east and south-west, where the Ibo and Yoruba peoples are respectively dominant.

Also in 1960, the former German colony of Cameroons, now under French and British trusteeship, will pass out of trusteeship. The larger, French, part is to become a sovereign state; the British parts may opt to remain linked with Nigeria.

Ghana and Nigeria produce nearly half the world's cocoa, a valuable dollar earner. Ghana's bauxite may become the basis for a big aluminium industry if the Volta River scheme for hydro-electric power and other development is fully carried out.

37

FRANCE AND AFRICA

In September 1958 the new French government of General de Gaulle (*38*) offered to all French territories overseas (except Algeria) a new form of association with France as largely self-governing republics, and at the same time a chance to vote themselves into full independence. In the referendum, the people of French Guinea voted for independence, and it immediately became a sovereign state.

All the other territories voted to become republics within the new French 'community'. Ubangui later adopted the name of 'Central African Republic'. In 1959 Senegal and French Sudan agreed to form a federation called Mali. Guinea had already agreed to federate itself with Ghana (*36*), but it was not clear how close these links would become. With Nigeria and Cameroons due to become independent in 1960, further regroupings of West African states may be expected.

France's reasons for retaining Algeria (*38*), whatever happens in other parts of Africa, have been reinforced by the discovery of iron ore around Tindouf and, in 1956, of several oilfields of great promise in the Saharan 'southern territories'. The French have built pipelines to bring out this oil in quantities that will reduce their dependence on Middle East oil; they hope to bring out 8 million tons in 1960, 25 million a year by 1965.

But Sahara oil has to come out through war-torn Algeria, or through Tunisia or Libya, which sympathize with the Algerian rebels. And Moroccan nationalists are now laying claim to the Tindouf area, and even to Mauritania—a desert territory whose few inhabitants do in fact look northward to the Arab world rather than south to Negro Africa.

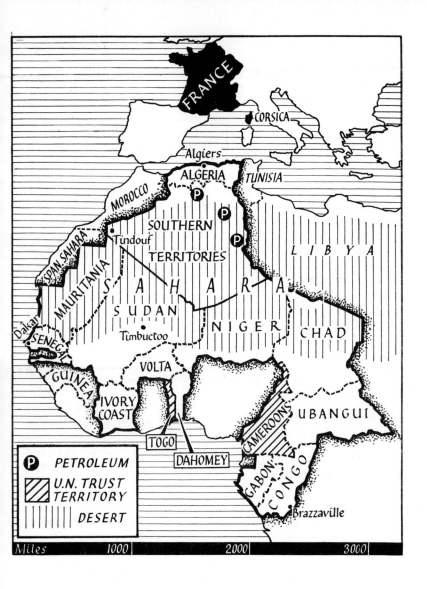

FRANCE

CORSICA

Algiers

MOROCCO

ALGERIA   TUNISIA

SPAN. SAHARA

P

SOUTHERN

Tindouf   P

TERRITORIES   P   L I B Y A

MAURITANIA   S   A   H   A   R   A

S U D A N

Dakar   N I G E R   CHAD

SENEGAL   Timbuctoo

GUINEA   VOLTA

IVORY   CAMEROONS   U B A N G U I
COAST

TOGO

DAHOMEY   GABON   C O N G O

Brazzaville

P	PETROLEUM
⧄	U.N. TRUST TERRITORY
⦀	DESERT

Miles   1000   2000   3000

83

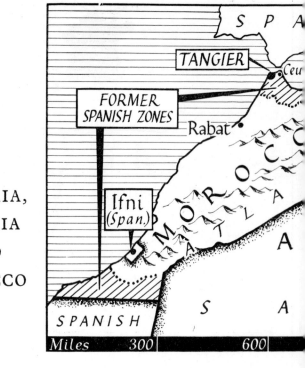

38

**ALGERIA,
TUNISIA
AND
MOROCCO**

In May and June 1958 the 400,000-strong French army in Algeria, weary with three years' unsuccessful efforts to crush the Arab rebels there, and backed by French civilians in Algeria and many in France itself, defied its own government and forced it to hand over power to General de Gaulle, the national hero of 1940–44. De Gaulle created a strong new regime in France (the Fifth Republic), but found no immediate way of ending the war in Algeria.

France had conquered Algeria in the 1830s, and since 1881 its northern districts had been considered as part of France. Nearly a million of Algeria's nine million inhabitants are French, and they have demanded full integration with France as uncompromisingly as the rebels have demanded full independence.

Tunisia and Morocco, on the other hand, became independent states in 1956. Tunisia had been a French protectorate since 1881. Morocco had been divided, in 1912, into French and Spanish zones,

Tangier becoming an international zone. After 1945 agitation for independence increased, backed by guerrilla fighting, and in 1954 France embarked on negotiations which led to settlements in both countries. During 1956 Spain's northern zone and Tangier also reverted to Moroccan rule; but up to 1959 the Spanish position in the south, and in Ceuta and Melilla, was uncertain, and Spain insisted that Ifni was legally Spanish.

Tunisia and Morocco support the Algerian rebels, as fellow Arabs; so their new relations with France have been uneasy. A particularly tense moment came in February 1958 when the French bombed Sakiet, a Tunisian village on the border. French resentment at Egyptian support for the rebels contributed to the 1956 Suez conflict (44). But the Arab *Maghreb* ('West') as a whole is more western-minded than Egypt, and in early 1959 Tunisia was sharply at odds with Egypt.

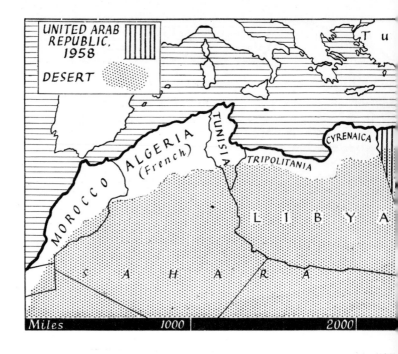

UNITED ARAB
REPUBLIC.
1958

DESERT

MOROCCO
ALGERIA
(French)
TUNISIA
TRIPOLITANIA
CYRENAICA
L I B Y A
S A H A R A

Miles   1000   2000

39

ARAB UNITY AND DISUNITY

Egypt and Syria merged in February 1958 to form the United Arab
Republic (*45*), to which Yemen also loosely attached itself. This was
the first, and so far the only, definite advance toward political union
in the Arab world.

The Arabic language links 85 million people, not all of Arab stock;
the Moslem religion, centred on Mecca, is another link, although
Lebanon is half Christian. But Arab nationalism is also largely a
common reaction against foreign rule. In the 1920s, after the collapse of the Turkish Ottoman empire which had once dominated
the Arab world, Morocco, Algeria, Tunisia, Syria, and Lebanon
were under French control, and Libya under Italian, while Britain
controlled Egypt, Sudan, Palestine, Transjordan (*40*), Iraq, Aden,
Oman, and the Persian Gulf sheikhdoms (*45*). Only Iraq and Egypt

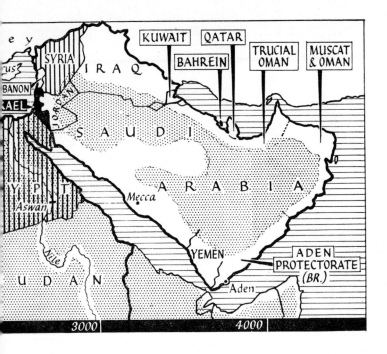

attained independence in the 1930s, and it was qualified by military treaties with Britain. But between 1944 and 1956, Syria, Lebanon, Jordan, Libya, Sudan, Morocco, and Tunisia gained independence. They are now all loosely linked with Egypt, Iraq, Saudi Arabia, and Yemen in the Arab League. French control is thus limited to Algeria (*38*), British to Aden, Oman, and the Gulf sheikhdoms.

Egypt, far the most populous (24 million) of the Arab states, has claimed the leadership of the 'Arab movement' since Colonel Nasser and other officers seized power in Egypt in 1952. Common hostility to Israel (*40, 44*) united the Arabs; and all support, with varying degrees of enthusiasm, the campaign to oust France and Britain from their positions. But the Sudan has withstood Egyptian pressure for 'unity of the Nile valley', and has doubts about Nasser's project for a huge Nile dam at Aswan; and Tunisia and Morocco (*38*), Lebanon, Jordan, Saudi Arabia, and Iraq (*45, 46*) each have special viewpoints which differ from Egypt's.

40

ISRAEL

Palestine, formerly part of the Turkish empire, was ruled by Britain from 1918 to 1948 under a League of Nations mandate which provided that a Jewish 'national home' should be created there without injury to the Arab population. But when persecution in Nazi Germany accelerated Jewish migration to Palestine, hostility between Arabs and Jews boiled up. After the Nazis' wartime massacre of millions of Jews, Zionism—the movement for a return to the Jews' ancestral homeland—gained wider support, particularly in America. Britain, trying to curb illegal immigration and mounting violence by both Jewish and Arab guerrillas, was bitterly criticized by both parties' supporters abroad. In 1947 it announced that it would withdraw from Palestine the next year, and invited the United Nations to tackle the problem.

The UN Assembly adopted a plan, backed by America and Russia, to divide Palestine into Jewish and Arab states, with Jerusalem internationalized. But the Arabs rejected the plan and the UN provided no means of carrying it out. As soon as Britain withdrew in May 1948 the Jews proclaimed the new state of Israel, which America and Russia quickly recognized; but they were at once attacked from all sides by the neighbouring Arab states.

The Israelis, although greatly outnumbered, fought back desperately, and when UN mediation eventually secured a set of armistice agreements in 1949 they were left in control of more territory than the 1947 partition plan had allotted them, including part of Jerusalem. Transjordan annexed the hill country of central Palestine and renamed itself Jordan. Egypt kept control of the Gaza strip. Most of the former Arab inhabitants of Israel had become refugees in Gaza, Jordan, Syria, and Lebanon, existing on UN funds mainly given by Britain and America. The Arab states refused to recognize Israel's existence or make peace with it. They blockaded it on three sides, and border raids and Israeli retaliations continued, despite the efforts of UN truce teams, until the more serious conflict of 1956 (*44*).

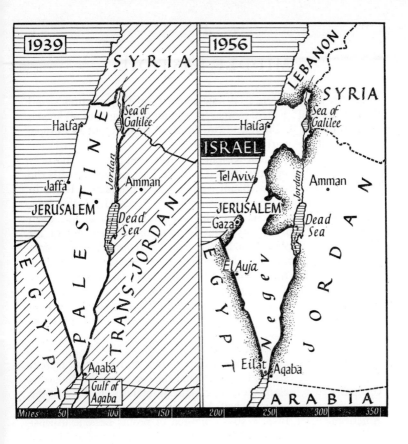

89

41

MIDDLE EAST OIL

A quarter of the world's oil now comes from the countries round the Persian Gulf, which, moreover, contain two-thirds of all known reserves of oil (3). They send two-thirds of their output to Europe, supplying three-quarters of its needs.

The tiny Sheikhdom of Kuwait (45), where oil began to flow only in 1945, has become the biggest Middle East producer, with the biggest known reserves. Saudi Arabia, where production began in 1939, ranks second, and the older sources, Persia (Iran) and Iraq, third and fourth. Persia's output, beginning in 1912, had risen to 32 million tons by 1950; but in 1951 the government of Dr Mossadegh expropriated the British-owned company, Anglo-Iranian, and seized its refinery at Abadan and other installations. Deadlock followed, Britain failing to get redress, and Persia, unable to work the installations or sell the oil, suffering from loss of revenue and unemployment. In 1953 Mossadegh's political opponents ousted him, and the new government agreed that, while the Anglo-Iranian installations would remain nationalized, a group of experienced oil companies would run them on Persia's behalf.

This 'consortium' in Persia comprises British, American, Dutch, and French interests. In Iraq and Qatar the companies holding concessions also represent these four national interests. In Kuwait the concession is half British, half American; in Saudi Arabia, wholly American. After 1951, a 50–50 division of profits became usual—half to the companies and half to the local governments; but the governments now show signs of pressing for more than half.

About two-thirds of Middle East oil is shipped from Persian Gulf ports, mainly through the Suez Canal (42). But some 40 million tons a year is piped to Lebanese and Syrian ports on the Mediterranean, through pipelines from the Saudi and northern Iraq fields—although the Arabs have blocked the line to Haifa in Israel since the Palestine war of 1948 (40). In 1956 the obstruction of the canal and Syria's temporary blocking of the other Iraq pipelines stimulated plans for new pipelines.

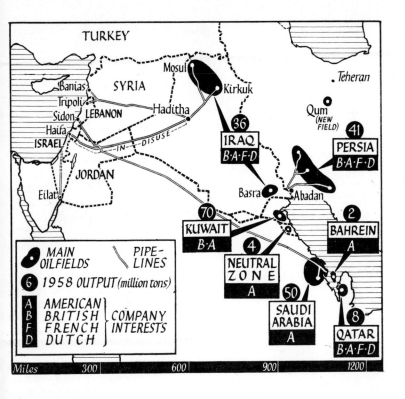

TURKEY

Mosul
Kirkuk

SYRIA

Banias
Tripoli
Sidon LEBANON   Haditha
Haifa
ISRAEL   —IN-DISUSE—

JORDAN

Eilat

. Teheran

Qum
(NEW FIELD)

(36)
IRAQ
B·A·F·D

(41)
PERSIA
B·A·F·D

Basra   Abadan

(70)
KUWAIT
B·A

(2)
BAHREIN
A

(4)
NEUTRAL
ZONE
A

(50)
SAUDI
ARABIA
A

(8)
QATAR
B·A·F·D

MAIN
OILFIELDS   PIPE-
LINES

(6) 1958 OUTPUT (million tons)

A AMERICAN
B BRITISH   } COMPANY
F FRENCH   INTERESTS
D DUTCH

Miles   300   600   900   1200

91

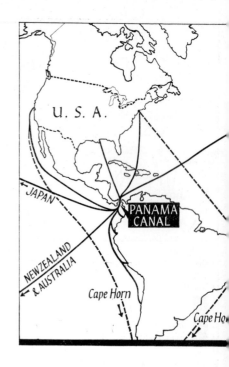

42

SUEZ AND PANAMA TRAFFIC

About 120 million tons of seaborne cargo, a sixth of the world total, pass through the Suez Canal in a normal year, as against 45 million through the Panama Canal. Half the Suez traffic is oil; half of western Europe's oil, and three-quarters of Britain's, comes that way. A quarter of Britain's whole trade is via Suez, and a quarter of all Suez traffic is British. But most European trading countries are also heavily dependent on the canal, as are, too, India, Pakistan, Malaya, Australia, and other Indian Ocean countries, and of course the Middle East oil-producing states themselves.

Until 1956 it was expected that Suez traffic would go on increasing rapidly for many years. The canal company, which had already tripled the width and doubled the depth of the canal, was planning

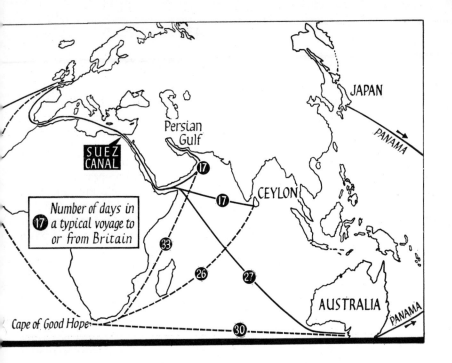

Number of days in a typical voyage to or from Britain

further enlargements. Experts believed that by 1965 200 million tons of oil a year might be coming westwards from the Middle East, and by 1975 450 million. But when the future of the canal became uncertain, attention was turned to projects for building new pipelines, and super-tankers which could carry oil relatively cheaply round the Cape of Good Hope.

Panama Canal traffic has been increasing more slowly, and is not expected to rise above 60 million tons a year during this century. Two-thirds of it goes to or from the United States, and one-sixth consists of shipments between the U.S. Pacific and Atlantic coasts. Built (between 1904 and 1914), operated, and guarded by the United States, to which the republic of Panama has granted permanent and quasi-sovereign authority over a zone extending five miles from each bank, the canal contains locks which make it more vulnerable than Suez to sabotage or surprise attack. If it were closed, much of its traffic might be sent overland rather than right round Cape Horn in the far south.

43

SUEZ HISTORY

The issues and emotions involved in the Suez Canal conflict of 1956 reflected a century of history. The canal was built between 1859 and 1869 by an international company based in France. The Turkish Sultan and his Viceroy in Egypt granted the company a concession until 1968. At first Britain opposed the scheme, fearing that its Indian empire would be endangered if other European powers got easier access to the Indian Ocean. But, once built, the canal soon replaced the sea route round the Cape of Good Hope as Britain's imperial 'life-line'. Britain bought an interest in the canal company in 1875, and in 1882 occupied Egypt, completing a strategic chain whose other links were Gibraltar, Malta, and Aden.

Protection of this 'life-line' became a British preoccupation. Russia, whose conquests in Asia threatened India directly, also tried to thrust through the Balkans and Turkey to the Mediterranean; Britain's counter-measures included the occupation of Cyprus (31). Germany, before and during the first world war, sought direct access to the Persian Gulf through Turkey; after the war Britain, having driven the Turks out of Iraq and Palestine, retained these territories under League of Nations mandates. In the 1939–45 war Germany, attacking through North Africa, came near to the canal itself before being beaten back. Then, between 1944 and 1948, Russia gained control of the Balkans (15), threatened Turkey, and tried to turn Greece and northern Persia into satellite states.

During the war Britain had built up a big military base alongside the canal, and this base, accessible by sea from south and north, seemed the natural hub for a new defence system to secure the Middle East against Russia. But Egypt insisted on evacuation of the base by 1956 in accordance with the 1936 Anglo-Egyptian treaty, and in June 1956 the last British troops duly left. By then the Baghdad Pact (46) had created a new defensive alliance along Russia's southern flank. But Egypt's pan-Arab ambitions and hostility to any alignment with the West had brought it to a degree of dependence on Russia which aroused fears of Russia getting an indirect grip on the canal. With the advance to independence of India, Pakistan, Ceylon, and Burma (9, 10, 47), the 'life-line' had lost its old imperial character. But the canal was still a strategic link between Britain and

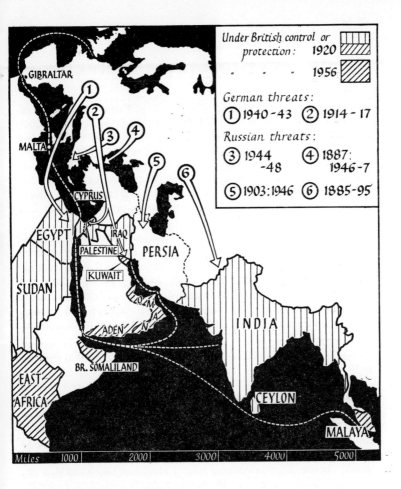

Under British control or protection: 1920

"   "   "   1956

German threats:
① 1940-43   ② 1914-17

Russian threats:
③ 1944   ④ 1887:
   -48   1946-7

⑤ 1903:1946   ⑥ 1885-95

Miles 1000   2000   3000   4000   5000

Malaya, East Africa, Australia, and New Zealand; and it had taken on
a new importance with the great increase in British and European
dependence on oil from the Persian Gulf (*3*, *41*, *42*).

44

THE 1956 SUEZ-SINAI CONFLICT

In July 1956 America and Britain withdrew their offer to help finance Egypt's plan for a huge dam at Aswan on the Nile (39). President Nasser's retort was the summary expropriation of the Suez Canal Company. He promised to respect the 1888 convention which guaranteed free passage, but his intentions were deeply distrusted by Britain, France, and other important canal users. In September Egypt rejected an 18-nation proposal for an international regime for the canal, and in October Russia vetoed it in the UN Security Council.

A few days later a joint military command aimed against Israel was agreed to by Egypt, Syria, and Jordan. Israel, already alarmed by Egypt's acquisitions of aircraft and tanks from Russia, then invaded Sinai on October 29th, swiftly routing the Egyptians and nearing the canal. Next day Britain and France demanded to be allowed to occupy key points along the canal. When Egypt refused, Britain and France bombed Egyptian airfields, and on November 5th their troops seized Port Said. A few hours later all four belligerents ceased fire. By then Egypt had blocked the canal by sinking 40 ships in it.

The UN Assembly demanded almost unanimously that Britain, France, and Israel withdraw, and an international UN force of about 6,000 men was organized to help avert further conflict. The British and French withdrew in December; and in January Israel evacuated most of Sinai. It held on to the Gaza strip and the Gulf of Aqaba coast, but declared itself ready to give up these areas too if the UN would prevent Egypt resuming border raids and its blockade of the gulf, and barring the canal to Israeli trade. But in March political and economic pressure forced Israel to pull out without any definite guarantees.

By April 1957 the canal was cleared and in use; and the original problems reappeared. Egypt insisted on full control of the canal, including the right to bar Israeli trade. The Arab states as a whole still refused to make peace with Israel. Egypt and Saudi Arabia said they would resume blockading the Gulf of Aqaba; but in fact ships have since then continued to get through to the long-blockaded port of Eilat, their cargoes including oil for the pipeline which Israel had

quickly built northward to Beersheba. However, the small UN force
on the Gaza–Eilat armistice line and near Sharm el Sheikh helped
to avert a fresh conflict there. In 1959 the UN force was still there;
and its presence had helped to stabilize the area during the crises of
1958 (45).

45

THE ARABS IN 1958, AND AFTER

After Syria's merger with Egypt in the United Arab Republic (*39*) in February 1958, pro-UAR groups in Lebanon revolted, and their government complained to the United Nations that the UAR was helping the rebels. UN observers went to the Lebanon–Syria border. Meanwhile Iraq and Jordan (*40*, *46*) had formed a rival Arab union; but in July Iraqi army officers overthrew the monarchy and the pro-western government. Lebanon and Jordan then appealed for immediate military help from America and Britain, and American troops were rushed to Beirut, British troops to Amman. These forces were not called on to fight, and in October they withdrew by agreement. By then the new Iraqi government seemed stabilised; a compromise government had been formed in Lebanon; and a UN mission had been placed in Jordan to report any fresh threat by its neighbours.

Jordan—which in 1957 had ended its alliance with Britain—now seems precariously sustained by the balance of forces between Israel, the UAR, and the new Iraq; for Iraq, being no longer allied to the West (*46*), has become Egypt's rival among the Arab states in a new sense.

Britain, although it has thus lost its only Arab ally, is still involved in Arabia politically. It controls Aden and the Aden protectorate (which Yemen claims); and the 'oil sheikhdoms' of Kuwait, Bahrein, and Qatar (*41*), the seven little sheikhdoms of Trucial Oman, and the sultanate of Muscat and Oman are 'protected states' bound to Britain by old treaties made long before the oil boom. Arab nationalism, fostered by UAR propaganda, is stirring in these areas, which may soon yield further crises. (The sultan of Muscat and Oman has already contended with two recent revolts.) Britain has also been embroiled with Saudi Arabia since 1952 over the disputed Buraimi oasis, on the border between Muscat and Trucial Oman. Saudi Arabia, however, has been vastly enriched by American oil royalties, and provides America with an air base at Dhahran; and its king, like Jordan's, has no love for Egypt's republican ideas.

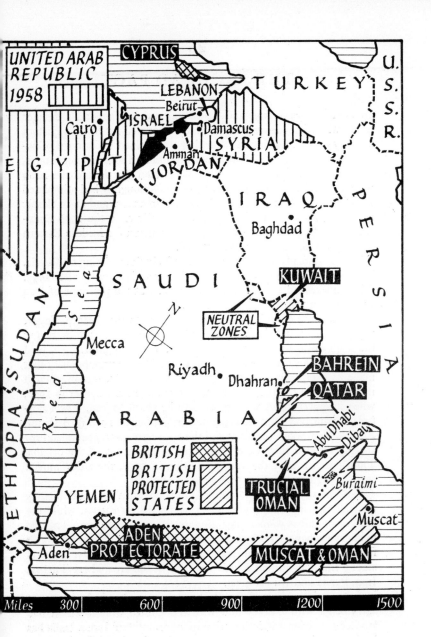

UNITED ARAB
REPUBLIC
1958

CYPRUS

TURKEY

U.
S.
S.
R.

LEBANON
Beirut
ISRAEL
Cairo
Damascus
Amman
SYRIA
JORDAN

EGYPT

IRAQ
Baghdad

SAUDI

KUWAIT

NEUTRAL
ZONES

PERSIA

Mecca

Riyadh
Dhahran

BAHREIN
QATAR

ARABIA

AbuDhabi
Dibai

BRITISH
BRITISH
PROTECTED
STATES

TRUCIAL
OMAN

Buraimi

YEMEN

Muscat

ETHIOPIA
SUDAN

Red Sea

ADEN
PROTECTORATE
Aden

MUSCAT & OMAN

Miles   300   600   900   1200   1500

99

46

THE BAGHDAD PACT

In February 1955 Iraq and Turkey signed in Baghdad a defence treaty which they invited other states concerned for Middle Eastern security to join. During the year they were joined by Britain, Pakistan, and Persia (Iran). Thus a 'northern tier' of four Moslem states, backed by Britain, came into being between Russia and the Arab world. America did not join the alliance (although it had stimulated the idea of the 'northern tier'), but it became more and more closely associated with the Baghdad Pact, especially after the 1956 Suez–Sinai conflict (44), when it declared its concern for Middle Eastern security in the 'Eisenhower Doctrine'.

Turkey (already a Nato ally) and Persia, both bordering on Russia, had both been subjected to Russian threats and pressures after 1945. Their interest in the alliance was simple. But the positions of Iraq and Pakistan were more complicated.

Iraq was the only Arab country belonging to the alliance. Egypt, supported by much Arab opinion elsewhere, accused it of betraying the Arab world by siding with the West. The Iraq government held firm, but its loyalty to its allies contributed to the unpopularity that made its overthrow in 1958 so easy (45). (Similarly, Jordan, though it never joined the Baghdad Pact, suffered internal disorder in 1956, when its government was reported to be about to join. The Palestinians who had been incorporated in Jordan in 1948 (40) shared Egypt's view about the Pact, and the 1956 riots clearly revealed how sharply divided they were from most of the Arabs of the original Transjordan.) After the Iraq revolution in 1958, the allies moved their headquarters offices to Ankara.

Early in 1959, the new military government in Iraq was bitterly quarrelling with Egypt, and being supported by Russia, while the local communists were also gaining in strength inside Iraq. This led to angry exchanges between Egypt and Russia too. There were also fears that Russia and the Iraqi communists would foster a revolt among the four million Kurds who live in the area where Turkey, Iraq, Persia and Russia meet.

When Pakistan joined the Baghdad Pact it already had defence agreements with Turkey and with the United States, which had aroused suspicion and indignation in 'uncommitted' India. India has incessantly denounced the pact, and Pakistan's other defensive links,

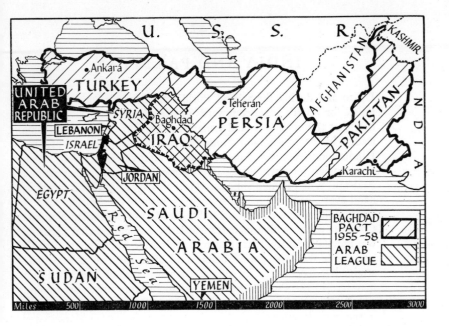

including the South-East Asia treaty (*55*), as being aimed against India, and has used their existence as an argument for holding on to Kashmir (*48*).

47

INDIA AND PAKISTAN

Up to and during the second world war, Britain's successive proposals for India's advance towards independence were based on the idea that the country would remain united. But in the 1940s some leaders of the 100-million strong Moslem minority, fearful of what Hindu dominance would mean for them after the British left, began to campaign for a wholly separate Moslem state which they named Pakistan. When Britain announced in February 1947 that it meant to hand over power in a matter of months, most of the Moslem leaders quickly plumped for Pakistan, and the leaders of the Indian National Congress party (which includes Moslems) recognized that partition was inevitable unless there was to be full-scale war after the British left. As it was, the period before and after the two new nations attained independence in August 1957 was one of bloodshed and massacre in the Punjab, Bengal, and some other areas; six million people migrated from India to Pakistan and a corresponding number in the opposite direction.

As far as possible the division was made on the basis of self-determination by majority vote or similar means, but some 40 million Moslems remained in India and 10 million Hindus in Pakistan. Pakistan took shape as two widely separated areas, each containing about half of its total population (about 80 million, as against post-partition India's 380 million). Relations between its two wings are not always good, the Bengalis often suspecting that the capital, Karachi, favours the western half unduly. Relations between Pakistan and India have been clouded since 1947 by the exodus of Hindus, victims of or afraid of persecution, from East Bengal; by claims and counter-claims to property abandoned by refugees; by disputes over the waters of the big Punjab rivers; and above all by the quarrel over Kashmir (48).

In October 1958 Pakistan's attempts to create a parliamentary democracy broke down, and the army seized power. This naturally made India particularly anxious, but both governments behaved cautiously, and no immediate trouble followed.

48

KASHMIR

When India and Pakistan became independent in 1947, the departing British urged all rulers of princely states (51) to accede to one or the other, but the maharaja of Kashmir did not. His rule was unpopular even among his fellow Hindus, and three-quarters of his four million subjects were Moslems. When the British left in August, his troops were already fighting Moslem rebels, and in October about 3,000 Pathan tribesmen from the North-West Frontier, abetted by some Pakistani officials, attacked Kashmir. The maharaja fled, appealing to India for help and offering to accede to it. Indian troops were rushed in, but although the Pathans soon went home the Kashmiri Moslems were now up in arms in the west and north, and during 1948 Pakistan sent troops in to prevent India from subduing them. British officers still serving with both armies tried to limit the fighting, and in January 1949 a cease-fire was agreed under United Nations auspices.

The UN had been invoked by India, which accused Pakistan of aggression. Pakistan pointed out that India had promised to let the Kashmiris decide their own fate by plebiscite. India repeated this promise but insisted that Pakistan must withdraw its troops first. By 1952, UN efforts to get agreement about the timing and scale of troop withdrawals had run into deadlock. In 1956 India announced that Kashmir was now irrevocably Indian territory (an attitude encouraged by Russia). But, while India's nominal claims were now extended to Chitral too, it offered to settle for the existing cease-fire line. Pakistan still pressed for a plebiscite. In 1957, when India was completing the constitutional absorption of Kashmir, the UN Security Council ruled that this was invalid. At the same time Pakistan asked that a UN force be sent to replace both armies in Kashmir, offering, if India was unwilling, to withdraw unilaterally and let a UN force garrison 'Azad Kashmir' (the north and west).

U.S.S.R.   CHINA

CEASE-FIRE ◆◆◆◆
LINE

Chitral

Gilgit

PAKISTAN

Muzaffarabad

Ladakh

Srinagar

Poonch

Jammu

Jhelum

INDIA

Lahore Amritsar

Miles   100   200   300   400

49

AFGHANISTAN

In 1947 Pakistan inherited from Britain the task of restraining the Pathan tribes of the North-West Frontier mountains from raiding the plains. The ruling dynasty in Afghanistan thought it saw an opportunity to extend its power. Pathans are the largest element in Afghanistan's mixed population of twelve million, and the Kabul dynasty had often tried to win the allegiance of the seven million other Pathans across the frontier fixed in 1893 (the 'Durand line'). It now launched a campaign of propaganda and subversion aimed at carving out a new state, 'Pakhtunistan' or 'Pathanistan', from Pakistani territory. But the tribesmen proved unenthusiastic, and the campaign drew little attention until in 1955 Russia came out in support of it. Russia's unconcealed aim was to frighten Pakistan into abandoning its alliances with western countries.

Earlier in 1955 Pakistan had been provoked, after a mob attack on its embassy in Kabul, into breaking off trade relations for a time, during which Afghanistan, deprived of its main trading channel through Karachi, found itself critically dependent on Russia. The Kabul government seemed to overlook the risk that the fostering of Pathan nationalism might completely disrupt Afghanistan, and that the Tajik, Uzbek, and Turkmen elements in its mixed population might gravitate towards their kinsmen in the adjacent republics of Soviet Central Asia. By 1957, however, a certain reconciliation had been achieved.

Miles 200 | 400 | 600 | 800 | 1000

50

GOA

When India became independent in 1947, it began pressing France and Portugal to cede the small possessions on or near its coasts which they had retained during many years of British rule. Chandernagore, on the Hooghly river above Calcutta, was handed over in 1951 after a local referendum. The other French enclaves—Pondicherry, Karakal, Mahé, and Yanam, totalling only 200 square miles with 300,000 inhabitants—were transferred to India in 1954 after their local councils had voted for the transfer.

Portugal, in contrast, declared that it was unthinkable to give up its territories. Indian indignation rose high, and angry official exchanges were accompanied by sporadic acts of violence. In August 1955 several thousand demonstrators tried to march into Goa, and a number of them were shot by frontier police. The Indian government discouraged further mass actions, but relations went on deteriorating, and during 1956 India cut off virtually all movement, trade, and communication across the border.

Goa (1,500 sq. miles, 550,000 inhabitants) is the only sizeable relic of Portuguese power in India; Daman and Diu (70,000 and 20,000 inhabitants) are mere vestigial fragments. The choice between India and Portugal is not easy for the many Goans who, on the one hand, are Catholic, have some Portuguese ancestry, and live as much in European as in Indian style; while, on the other, they have been accustomed to seek education and employment in India. India's economic restrictions cut off both trade and a yearly flow of about £4 million sent home by Goans working in India to support their families. Hitherto few Goans have shown much enthusiasm for union with India. Their attitude may change as they see the disappearance of the advantages (including smuggling) which their double connexion used to bring them. But, up to 1959, Portugal seemed in no mood to let the people of Goa decide their own future.

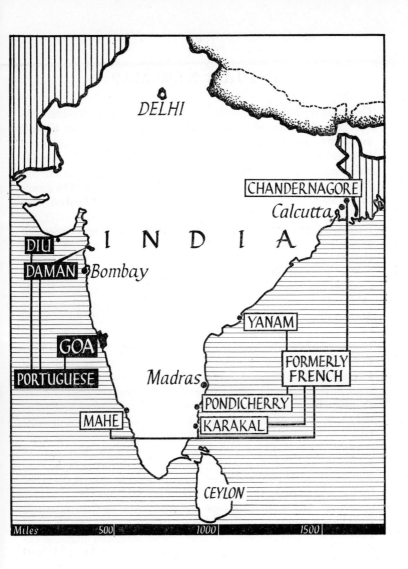

DELHI

CHANDERNAGORE
Calcutta

I N D I A

DIU
DAMAN • Bombay

YANAM

GOA
FORMERLY
FRENCH

PORTUGUESE
Madras

PONDICHERRY

MAHE
KARAKAL

CEYLON

Miles   500   1000   1500

51

INDIA'S NEW MAP

On attaining independence in 1947, India set out to liquidate the 600 princely states which Britain had allowed a degree of internal autonomy, and to reshape the old provinces so that each major language group would be administered as a unit. Most of the princely rulers resigned themselves to the absorption of their territories. The Moslem ruler of Junagadh, a small state in Kathiawar, tried to accede to Pakistan, but Indian troops took over his state. Hyderabad, with 17 million people, was a bigger nut to crack; its Moslem ruler, the Nizam, sought independent status. After a year of negotiation, an appeal by Hyderabad to the UN, and a blockade by India, Indian forces moved in and the Nizam capitulated.

The government then went ahead on the linguistic principle, creating the new states of Andhra (Telugu language) and Kerala (Malayalam), and adjusting the boundaries of Mysore (Kanarese); Madras (Tamil); Orissa (Oriya); West Bengal (Bengali); Bihar, Uttar and Madhya Pradesh, and Rajasthan (variants of Hindi). The Sikhs' claims for a separate province in East Punjab were rejected. So were those of the mountain peoples of Assam, and there was open revolt among the Naga hillmen from 1954 onwards. The worst problems arose in Bombay state, where Gujerati is the main language north of Bombay city, Marathi in the south, while both are spoken in the city; the eventual decision to have a bilingual state left both groups dissatisfied. The new state borders came into effect in November 1956.

South India now presents two problems. In the new state of Kerala, communists won control of the state government in the 1957 elections. And Madras and other southern areas have been disturbed by the plan to make Hindi India's chief official language.

In 1958 linguistic strife took a violent form in Ceylon, whose government sought to make Sinhalese, spoken by only two-thirds of Ceylon's 9 million people, the only official language. Fighting between Sinhalese and the 2 million Tamils (originally from Madras) led to the imposing of martial law and the arrest of the Tamil leaders.

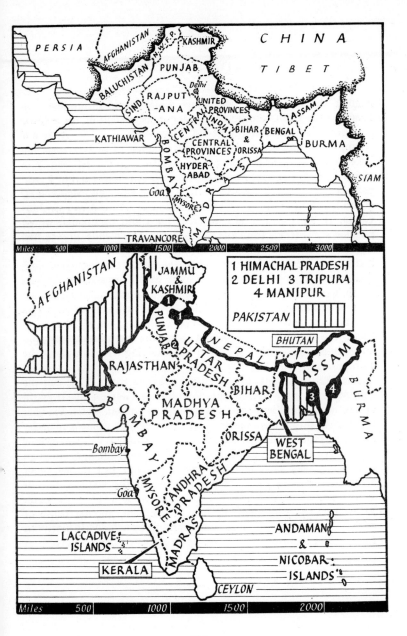

PERSIA
AFGHANISTAN
N.-F.P.
KASHMIR
CHINA
BALUCHISTAN
PUNJAB
TIBET
SIND
RAJPUT -ANA
Delhi
UNITED PROVINCES
ASSAM
KATHIAWAR
CENTRAL INDIA
BIHAR
BENGAL
BURMA
BOMBAY
CENTRAL PROVINCES
ORISSA
HYDER-ABAD
SIAM
Goa
MYSORE
MADRAS
TRAVANCORE

Miles 500 1000 1500 2000 2500 3000

1 HIMACHAL PRADESH
2 DELHI 3 TRIPURA
4 MANIPUR

PAKISTAN

AFGHANISTAN
JAMMU & KASHMIR
1
1
PUNJAB
UTTAR PRADESH
NEPAL
BHUTAN
ASSAM
RAJASTHAN
BIHAR
3
4
BURMA
MADHYA PRADESH
BOMBAY
ORISSA
Bombay
WEST BENGAL
Goa
MYSORE
ANDHRA PRADESH
ANDAMAN & NICOBAR ISLANDS
LACCADIVE ISLANDS
MADRAS
KERALA
CEYLON

Miles 500 1000 1500 2000

III

52

INDO-CHINA

Among the nationalist movements which rapidly developed in French Indo-China during the Japanese occupation of 1940–5, the strongest was the communist-led Viet Minh. France's post-war attempts to restore its authority led to a period of confused fighting interspersed with negotiation; and after the communist victory in China in 1949 the Viet Minh, now receiving Chinese military support, began to launch big attacks in Tonking, while also stepping up guerrilla action in the other Vietnamese areas, Annam and Cochin-China. In 1953–4 they also invaded Laos and Cambodia, whose peoples are distinct from the Vietnamese. Meanwhile France had begun a transfer of power to national governments in Laos, Cambodia, and Vietnam; but they remained within the French Union, and French troops were more and more heavily pressed by the Viet Minh, who in the spring of 1954 trapped a large force at Dien Bien Phu. A conference at Geneva, which opened just as Dien Bien Phu fell, brought agreement on a general cease-fire; on withdrawal of Viet Minh and French forces from Cambodia and most of Laos; and on withdrawal to either side of a line dividing Vietnam along the 17th parallel.

The French accordingly evacuated the Red River delta, and the Viet Minh set up a 'Democratic Republic of Vietnam' in Hanoi, in opposition to the Vietnamese government in Saigon. North Vietnam was turned into a communist state. In the south, where a majority of the 24 million Vietnamese live, the Republic of Vietnam is now wholly free of French control, as are Laos and Cambodia, although it relies heavily on American economic help. But it has never accepted the 1954 project for a reunion of the country by all-Vietnam elections, which could scarcely be free and fair in the north. As well as the continued division of Vietnam, another cause of anxiety was the communists' retention of strongholds in northern Laos; these, however, were given up in 1957.

53

MALAYA AND SINGAPORE

Malaya became the Commonwealth's tenth sovereign member in 1957. It had lagged behind politically in the post-war years. This was not simply because of the importance of its rubber and tin (*4*), or of Singapore's role as the trading hub of South-East Asia and the strategic key to the narrows between Indian Ocean and China Seas (Indonesia is also a major producer of tin and rubber, and commands the Sunda strait, an alternative link between the oceans). Malaya's special problem is its multiracial composition. Of the 8 million people of Malaya and Singapore, only 45 per cent. are Malays; a similar proportion are Chinese (*59*), who have flocked in since trade and tin began to develop under British rule; most of the remainder are Indians. In the past, Malays have been uneasy about the Chinese grip on trade and other economic activities. Today they are freshly concerned by the influence of a strong communist China. Communist Malayan Chinese launched in 1948 a guerrilla and terrorist campaign which tied down 20,000 troops. Even in 1959 some of them were still evading capture in Malaya's dense jungles; but they had failed to gain popular support.

Since 1948 mainland Malaya had been organized as a federation, comprising nine Malay sultanates and two coastal settlements, with Singapore as a separate colony. This reduced Malay fears of Chinese domination, for the separation of Singapore, four-fifths of whose $1\frac{1}{2}$ million inhabitants are Chinese, strengthened the Malays' position on the mainland. Mistrust was sufficiently overcome to enable a Malay–Chinese–Indian Alliance to win the federation's first fully democratic elections in 1955 and to form its first responsible government, which continued in office after 1957.

In Singapore too, despite periodic violence by communist-led groups, the 1955 constitution provided for a ministerial system and elective assembly. The new ministers' negotiations for *merdeka* (freedom) broke down in 1956 on the issue of Britain's right to intervene if the naval base was endangered by internal disorder; but further negotiations in 1957 produced an agreement for Singapore to become almost completely self-governing.

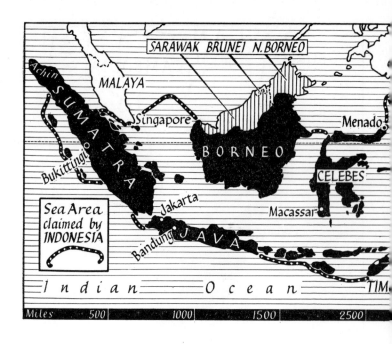

54

INDONESIA AND NEW GUINEA

In 1942 the Japanese overran the East Indian empire that Holland
had built up over three centuries. When Japan surrendered in 1945
the Dutch were unable to restore their authority over the huge archipelago's 80 million people. Nationalist leaders proclaimed a republic,
but found themselves struggling with local separatists as well as with
the Dutch. After much confused fighting and negotiation, a settlement was agreed with UN help and a sovereign Indonesia was recognized in 1949. All the former Dutch East Indies were assigned to the
new republic except western New Guinea (Irian), which was left in
Dutch hands pending negotiations on its fate. The failure of these
negotiations led to louder Indonesian demands for West Irian. Asian
opinion generally backed these demands, rejecting the argument that
the Papuans of New Guinea are not Indonesian and that the young
republic was already facing rebellions in Sumatra, Celebes, the

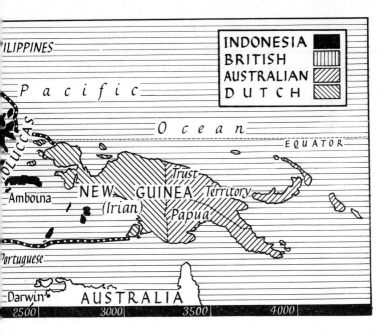

Moluccas, and even Java itself. In 1957 Indonesia expelled the remaining Dutch residents and seized Dutch property and enterprises. It also made a claim to the sea areas shown on the map, but did not enforce this claim immediately.

Australia, which controls eastern New Guinea, has been greatly concerned by the dispute. It wants Indonesian friendship, but also wants to see New Guinea in reliable hands, for the island is a stepping-stone for an attack on Australia, as Japan showed in 1942.

Two other parts of the archipelago remain under European rule—the Portuguese half of Timor, and the British parts of Borneo, whose future is linked with Malaya's (53). Indonesia has not extended its claims to them.

During 1957 strong separatist movements developed in Sumatra and Celebes, and in 1958 a rebel government was proclaimed at Bukittingi. The Indonesian government recaptured most of central Sumatra, but in 1959 the rebels were still resisting there and around Menado. They accused the government of giving too much power to communists.

55

DEFENCE IN SOUTH-EAST ASIA

The advance of communist military power from China southward into Indo-China (52) aroused alarm about the fate of all South-East Asia. Siam was most immediately threatened; but Indo-China is also only 250 miles from Malaya, and if it fell under communist control the road would lie open for further advances by way of Singapore and Indonesia, where there are large Chinese populations (59), towards Australia. Early in 1954, when the French defences in Indo-China were crumbling, western and Asian governments began to discuss the problem. Burma and Indonesia held to their neutralist policy of non-alliance, but in September 1954 Siam, the Philippines, and Pakistan (whose eastern wing would be threatened by any communist success in Burma) joined with America, Britain, France, Australia, and New Zealand in signing the Manila treaty for South-East Asian defence, usually dubbed 'Seato'.

The eight Seato allies agreed that they would act together against any attack on their territories in South-East Asia, or on Laos, Cambodia or South Vietnam, and that they would consult together if one of them believed any of these areas to be in danger. They explained that they would take no action on the territory of any of the Indo-Chinese states without its consent. Formosa and Hongkong were excluded from the terms of the treaty by a clause defining the area affected as south of latitude 21·30 north.

56

CHINA AND ITS NEIGHBOURS

Since the communists' victory in the Chinese civil war of 1947–9, China has become much the strongest Asian power, and a series of problems have arisen along its 2,500-mile-long eastern boundaries and coasts. Foremost is the problem of the rival Nationalist government in exile in Formosa (57), and the risk that America's commitment to support the Nationalists, and Russia's to support the communists, would convert any conflict across the Formosa strait into a world war. Formosa's fate is linked with Korea's (61, 62). Since communist China's intervention in Korea in 1950, Americans have regarded Formosa as an essential link in a chain of defence against further communist expansion in the Far East (64).

China now shares control of North Korea with Russia, and has regained from Russia the base at Port Arthur which enabled first Tsarist and later Soviet Russia to dominate the sea approaches to Peking. Southward along the coast, the European trading communities long established in Shanghai and other 'treaty ports' have been evicted by a series of 'squeezes', although Hongkong and Macao (58) still remain in foreign hands.

Japan and the Philippines are secured against any ambitions their newly powerful neighbour may cherish by defence treaties with America, which has kept bases in both countries (and in Okinawa), and by the sea. Korea lacks the protection of the sea; and so do China's neighbours in the south, the Indo-Chinese states, Siam and Burma (52, 55, 59). Burma has had to contend with irruptions across the border first by fugitive Nationalist Chinese and, more recently, by Chinese communist forces, as well as with a still unfinished guerrilla campaign waged by its own communists. India, in 1959, was disturbed by China's repression of the national rising in Tibet (60).

U. S. S. R.

MANCHURIA

OUTER MONGOLIA

Vladivostok

JAPAN

Anshan

KOREA

Pt. Arthur

Peking

Taku

SHANTUNG

N

CHINA

Yangtse

Shanghai

Okinawa

Ryukyu Is.

Chungking

Amoy

FORMOSA

Canton

HONGKONG (Br.)

VIETNAM

Hainan

PHILIPPINES

BURMA

LAOS

SIAM

Miles   500   1000   1500

57

FORMOSA AND QUEMOY

In 1949 Chiang Kai-shek and his defeated Nationalist government took refuge in Formosa (Taiwan) after the communists' victory in the Chinese civil war. Half a million Nationalist troops reached the island, whose population, predominantly Chinese, is about eight million. The Nationalists, who are still recognized as the lawful Chinese government by a majority of nations, regularly reaffirm their intention of returning to the mainland, while the Peking government equally regularly proclaims that it means to secure Formosa, preferably without needing to fight for it. In 1950, after the invasion of South Korea, America announced that its navy would cover the Formosa strait to prevent either of the rival governments from attacking each other. In 1953 this undertaking was changed into a one-way guarantee to defend Formosa, but subsequently Chiang was induced to promise that he would not attack the mainland against America's will.

The Nationalists still hold the Pescadores, and the Quemoy and Matsu islands near the mainland coast. In 1955 the communists began operations against the Tachen islands, and the Nationalist garrison there was withdrawn; but, deterred by American warnings, the communists did not assault the other 'offshore' islands, although Quemoy and Matsu lie embarrassingly close to the ports of Amoy and Foochow. Sporadic shelling of and from these islands continued, and on the mainland the communists built a number of airfields and a railway to Amoy which would improve their position if large-scale hostilities broke out.

In August 1958 the communists suddenly began an intense shelling of Quemoy, declared that their troops were about to land there, and demanded its surrender. But the Nationalists held firm, and after several weeks of tension Peking quietly backed down, confirming many people's suspicion that this episode was mainly a political gambit.

The future of the Nationalist government on Formosa, which depends heavily on American economic and military aid, remains uncertain; and while two rival Chinese governments continue to exist, there is also a clash of loyalties among the millions of Chinese settled in neighbouring Asian countries (59).

Shanghai

C H I N A

Tachen Is.

F U K I E N

Foochow • ← Matsu I.

F o r m o s a ___ S t r a i t

Taipeh

Amoy • ⬭ Quemoy I.

FORMOSA

Swatow • F o r m o s a

Pescadores

Miles | 100 | 200 | 300 | 400

58

HONGKONG AND MACAO

In the nineteenth century China's coast was speckled with European-ruled enclaves—Russian, German, British, French, and Portuguese —and with 'treaty ports' and 'concessions' where foreign trading communities enjoyed special rights. Today only Hongkong and Macao remain. Macao, settled by the Portuguese in the sixteenth century, is no longer a major trading centre, and its 150,000 inhabitants seem to survive mainly on subsidies from Portugal and the proceeds of gambling and speculation. Hongkong, in contrast, has flourished. The island—then barren—was annexed by Britain in 1841, and Kowloon in 1860, while the New Territories were obtained from China on a lease which runs to 1997. Hongkong's population, 99 per cent. of it Chinese, has been swollen to 2½ million by an influx of 800,000 refugees from the mainland since the civil war, and overcrowding is its worst problem. Its traditional trade was disrupted by communist China's drive for self-sufficiency and by the UN embargo imposed on China after its intervention in the Korean war (62), but its fine harbour has remained busy, and it has become a centre of manufacture supplying a wide area of the Far East.

China has made occasional threatening gestures in the direction of Hongkong and Macao, but on the whole has put remarkably little pressure on these colonial fragments. It suited the Peking government to keep this one door to the non-communist world ajar even during its period of near-isolation during the Korean war. Hongkong was also a lever which it could use to divide Britain from America, and a means of earning foreign currency. Peking seems content to see the British equip the little colony with installations which it expects one day to inherit intact. Although garrisoned, Hongkong could hardly be defended against a full-scale attack, and although it has lately become more self-sufficient it would be hard for it to survive a complete stoppage of supplies from the mainland.

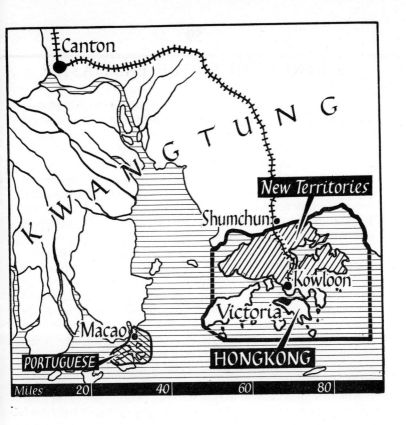

59

CHINESE IN SOUTH-EAST ASIA

Since 1950 the Chinese government in Peking and the rival Nationalist government in Formosa have competed for the loyalty of the 12 million Chinese settled in other countries. Most of these live in South-East Asia, although there are also Chinese communities in, for example, India, Africa, the West Indies, and the United States. Exact figures cannot be given; even where accurate censuses of population have been made, intermarriage and conflicting nationality laws make it difficult to say exactly who is Chinese and who is not. But the 'overseas Chinese' are numerically dominant in Singapore (53), and numerous in almost every South-East Asian centre of trade, mining, or industry. Even in a country like Indonesia, where they make up only about one-thirtieth of the whole population, their hold on trade, manufacturing, and other activities gives them a strong position. Although many of these Chinese have been settled abroad for generations, family links with their original homes, mostly in south China, are usually strong, and the political influence of Peking is powerful enough among them to worry most South-East Asian governments. Meanwhile, China's own population is now rising by about 12 million every year, and the Peking government is no longer trying to check this rapid increase.

A more limited cause of anxiety has been Peking's use of the Thai minority in south-western China as the basis for a 'Free Thai Movement', which might become a means of influencing the Thais and closely related peoples of Siam (Thailand), Laos, and the Shan states of eastern Burma.

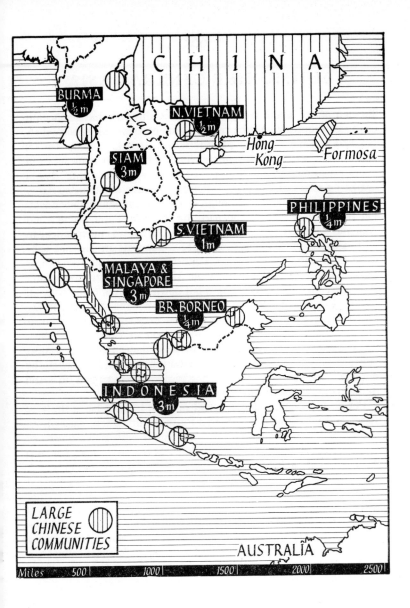

LARGE
CHINESE
COMMUNITIES

CHINA

BURMA
½m

N.VIETNAM
½m

Hong Kong

Formosa

SIAM
3m

Lao

PHILIPPINES
¼m

S.VIETNAM
1m

MALAYA &
SINGAPORE
3m

BR.BORNEO
¼m

INDONESIA
3m

AUSTRALIA

Miles 500 1000 1500 2000 2500

60

COMMUNIST CENTRAL ASIA

Russian and Chinese conquests in the eighteenth and nineteenth centuries subjugated all the central Asian peoples—Mongols, Tibetans, and Moslem Turki peoples (Turkmen, Uzbek, Kazakh, Tartar, and others), and drew an arbitrary line through their homelands, in effect partitioning central Asia. Between 1917 and 1922 Russia crushed a series of Turki liberation movements; and the Red Army also occupied Mongolia, although it is now nominally independent. On the Chinese side of the partition line the Turki peoples and Mongols were less firmly controlled, and Tibet was independent in all but name, until 1949–50. Chinese communist armies then subdued both Tibet and Chinese Turkistan (formerly also known as Sinkiang, but in 1955 renamed the Uighur—i.e. Turki—Region). Both the communist powers have put down Asian national revolts in recent years, and both have resorted to mass deportations; and the central Asian peoples' chances of independence are further diminishing as Russian and Chinese colonists flood into their homelands. There are now over 40 million Russian settlers in Asia, as against only six million in 1900; they already outnumber the Kazakhs in the nominally self-governing Kazakh area. Peking has plans to settle millions of Chinese in Mongol areas and Turkistan.

For both powers, this movement into the interior has a strategic value, and for China it is an outlet for over-population. Kazakhstan and other Turki areas have provided Russia with rich deposits of coal, oil, uranium, and other minerals. Since 1954 there has also been an intensive drive to grow more grain in their 'virgin lands'; but the climate is harsh, and little has come of the much-publicized plans to 'change nature' by reversing the flow of rivers and irrigating the deserts (one of the biggest of these projects, the Caspian–Aral canal, was quietly abandoned in 1954 after four years' work). The Turki and Kazakh areas of Central Asia have, however, provided Russia with sites for atomic weapon tests and rocket launching (*14*).

Since 1950 a new rail link between Russia and China has been built across Mongolia. A second railway, now being built across

Chinese Turkistan, has already reached the new oilfield near Yumen.

The Chinese have built two motor roads to Lhasa, and linked it with Peking by air services. During 1957–8, however, their plans were disrupted by a Tibetan guerrilla revolt, which began in the Chamdo area and spread west and south, coming close to the Himalayan passes into India. This has caused some uneasiness in India; so have recent Chinese attempts to win influence in Nepal and territory from Burma, and China's revival of old claims to parts of north-eastern India and of Ladakh in Kashmir (48). In March 1959 a general Tibetan revolt broke out in Lhasa itself, and Tibet's religious leader, the Dalai Lama, fled to India, where China's repressive action aroused widespread indignation.

61

KOREA AMONG THE GIANTS

Korea has long suffered from the habit that powerful nations have of regarding a smaller neighbour as a 'dagger pointed at our heart'. After centuries of Chinese domination it was slowly acquiring independence when in 1895 the Japanese moved in. In the war of 1905 Russia sought to break Japan's hold on the Korea Strait, the sea route to Russia's Far Eastern possessions; Japan's victory confirmed its hold on Korea and enabled it to penetrate Manchuria.

On Japan's surrender in 1945, America forces occupied southern Korea as well as Japan; but Russia, having declared war on Japan a week before the surrender, quickly sent troops into northern Korea. Although it was agreed that the military occupation should be temporary and that a united, free, and democratic Korean state should be set up, in the north the Russians, as in East Germany, installed a communist regime and crushed all opposition. Appeals from the UN Assembly were in vain, and a commission it sent to Korea was not allowed to enter the north. So in 1948 elections were held in South Korea only (where over two-thirds of the 30 million Koreans live) and a government was set up in the national capital, Seoul, with the UN's blessing. The Russian and American forces both withdrew, leaving the two rival governments facing each other in bitter hostility; and in 1950 the Korean war broke out (62).

Since the 1953 armistice North Korea has remained a kind of Russo-Chinese condominium, nominally independent but obedient to its big neighbours' wishes. In the south, the government headed by President Rhee has been far from docile. Although heavily dependent on American and UN economic aid and protection, its tough talk, while an understandable reaction to the continuing division of the country, has frequently alarmed or embarrassed its allies. Dr Rhee, who for thirty years was a leader of Korean resistance to Japanese rule, has also maintained an unfriendly attitude to Japan, and thus estranged Korea's only non-communist neighbour.

U. · S. · S. · R.

Sakhalin

MANCHURIA

C H I N A

Mukden·

Vladivostok·

Peking
·

Pt.Arthur

KOREA

JAPAN

Yellow
Sea

Seoul

Tokyo

Korea Strait

Nagasaki

·Shanghai

Miles   500   1000   1500

62

THE KOREAN WAR

In June 1950 the army of communist North Korea, equipped with Russian tanks, crossed the 38th parallel, which was then the dividing line between the two Korean states, at a dozen points. The UN Security Council at once demanded a withdrawal (no Soviet veto blocked this move, for Russia was boycotting the Council at the time). But the communists swept aside South Korea's lightly armed forces, reaching Seoul in two days. America announced that it would send forces to help resist the invasion, and the Council called on UN member nations to do the same. Within a few days 48 nations had backed the Council's decision, and 16 of them sent men to fight in Korea, the Commonwealth's contribution coming second to America's predominant one.

At first only a few American and Commonwealth units could get to Korea, and they and the South Koreans were forced back into a small area round Pusan. There they held out until mid-September, when fresh American forces landed at Inchon, freed Seoul and cut the communists' supply line. North Korea's army was driven back across the parallel, but it refused to negotiate. The UN allies paused, debating whether to pursue the aggressors and ensure that they would not strike again. A 47–5 vote in the UN Assembly authorized them to do so, and they crossed the parallel, capturing the communists' capital, Pyongyang, and shattering their army.

A few weeks later China sent into Korea a large army which drove the UN and South Korean forces far south, recapturing Seoul in January. The UN Assembly, failing to get China to agree to a cease-fire, declared it an aggressor, and later asked all member states to cut off trade with it. But the war was painstakingly limited to Korea, although this meant immunity from bombing for China's supply lines and bases just across the Yalu.

By June 1951 the allies had fought their way back to the parallel and the Chinese armies had suffered heavily. China then agreed to negotiations; but these, mainly at Panmunjom, dragged on for two years until an armistice was signed in July 1953. Most of the delay was caused by the communists' insistence that 50,000 prisoners-of-

war in UN hands must be handed back although they did not want to return to communist rule; in the end they were allowed to remain in South Korea or go elsewhere. A peace conference in 1954 brought no agreement, and Korea remains divided along the armistice line.

63

JAPAN'S LOST EMPIRE

Defeat in 1945 stripped Japan of the empire it had built up since 1895, when it took Formosa from China and made Korea a protectorate. In 1905 it had won from Russia the southern half of Sakhalin (Karafuto) and the China coast base of Port Arthur. From 1919 it held, under League of Nations mandate, the Mariana, Caroline, and Marshall islands, formerly a German colony. In 1931 it set up a puppet state in Manchuria, and in the next decade its armies conquered much of China proper. Finally, between 1940 and 1942 the Japanese overran or gained control of all South-East Asia, Indonesia, the Philippines, and other Pacific islands.

The earlier conquests were wiped out in 1945 as well as the wartime ones. China recovered Formosa (57). The Russians regained south Sakhalin, seized the Kuriles, and occupied North Korea (61) and Manchuria until local communists had got a grip. American forces occupied south Korea (until 1949) and the Ryukyu and Bonin islands, as well as Japan itself, where Commonwealth troops joined them.

In the peace treaty concluded in 1951 with all the world war allies except Russia and China, Japan renounced Formosa, Korea, Sakhalin, the Kuriles, and the mandated islands (which became an American trust territory under the UN), and agreed to provisional US administration of the Bonins and Ryukyus, including Okinawa (64). While the allied occupation of Japan itself was ended, Japan gave the United States the right to keep forces there for joint defence.

Japanese opinion took these losses quietly except for the Kuriles and Ryukyus. In 1956 the Russians flatly rejected all idea of returning even the southernmost Kurile islands, Kunashiri and Etorofu, but promised to hand back the tiny nearby islands of Shikotan and Habomai if and when a Russo-Japanese peace treaty could be concluded. They made it clear that first Japan must get the Americans out of the Ryukyus and Japan itself.

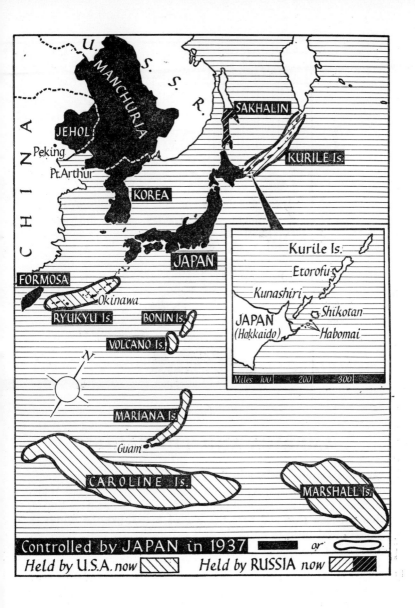

U. S. S. R.

MANCHURIA

JEHOL
Peking
Pt.Arthur

KOREA

CHINA

SAKHALIN

KURILE Is.

JAPAN

FORMOSA

Okinawa
RYUKYU Is.   BONIN Is.

VOLCANO Is.

N

Kurile Is.

Etorofu

Kunashiri

JAPAN
(Hokkaido)

Shikotan

Habomai

Miles 100   200   300

MARIANA Is.

Guam

CAROLINE Is.

MARSHALL Is.

Controlled by JAPAN in 1937 ▬▬ or ⬭

Held by U.S.A. now ⟍⟍⟍⟍   Held by RUSSIA now ⟋⟋⟋

64

AMERICA AND THE PACIFIC

America's strong position in the Pacific is a post-war phenomenon. In the nineteenth century the Americans opened Japan up to trade, annexed Hawaii and the Philippines and bought Alaska from Russia. But between 1920 and 1940 the United States, like the European powers, did little to check Japan's expansion. In 1941, however, everything was changed by the Japanese attack on the Philippines and on the U.S. naval base at Pearl Harbour in the Hawaii islands. The Americans fought their way back across the Pacific, with Australian and British help, until Japan itself surrendered in 1945. They then found themselves unchallenged in Pacific waters, but increasingly committed to protecting peoples and areas along the ocean's further shores.

The United States has retained control of the Mariana, Marshall, and Caroline islands as a UN trust territory, and of the Ryukyus and Bonins, now under provisional administration. It has mutual defence agreements with the Philippines (independent since 1946), South Korea, Japan, the Chinese Nationalists in Formosa, and South Vietnam (but in this last case it does not have the use of bases). In 1951 it joined Australia and New Zealand in the Pacific Security Treaty (often called the Anzus treaty); and in 1954 the three Anzus allies, with Britain, France, Pakistan, the Philippines, and Siam, signed the South-East Asia Collective Defence Treaty, usually known as Seato (55).

While most of these American commitments have arisen from fear of communist China and Russia, fear of possible Japanese revival has also played a part, as in the Anzus treaty.

65

THAWING CANADA'S NORTH

The scale of Canada's recent development has been prodigious. Its industries now produce more than twice as much as in 1939, since when its population has risen from 11 to 16½ million. Its industrial revolution has changed the face even of such conservative provinces as Quebec and New Brunswick. But since 1945 the pace has been hottest in the bleak north, in the three-quarters of all Canada where only 200,000 people inhabit 2¼ million square miles. On the Pacific coast mountain water power has been harnessed to create the world's second biggest aluminium industry at Kitimat. Rich uranium deposits have been exploited near Port Radium and Beaverlodge, as well as near Elliot Lake in the Algoma area of Ontario. In the Yukon the mining of base metals is eclipsing the old 'gold rushes'; and lead and zinc have also been found in plenty across Great Slave Lake from the gold town of Yellowknife. In northern Manitoba a new railway to Lynn Lake brings south 8,000 tons of nickel a year to supplement the Sudbury fields, which long provided four-fifths of the world's nickel. The oilfields found in Alberta since the Leduc strike in 1947 have multiplied Canadian petroleum output tenfold; and over 16 million million cubic feet of natural gas has been found with the oil.

On the Quebec–Labrador border 400 million tons of iron ore has been proved in the Knob Lake area, and a 360-mile railway has been built through the wilderness to get the ore to a new port at Seven Islands. The shipment of ore from Quebec, and from other countries, to the steel centres of the mid-western United States and Canada will now be easier and cheaper with the opening of the St Lawrence Seaway in 1959. As well as providing hydro-electric power for both countries, this $900 million Canadian–American project now enables ocean-going ships of 10,000 tons to reach the Great Lakes with cargoes for Ontario and the U.S. Mid-West. Before, only ships drawing less than 14 feet could navigate the hundred miles between Montreal and Lake Ontario.

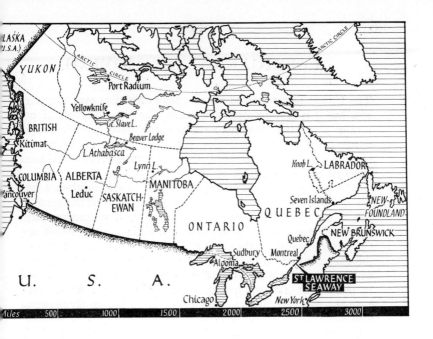

66

AMERICANS STILL MOVING

The United States marked out its present frontiers over a century ago, but it is still growing at a spectacular pace, not beyond but within them. Its population, absorbing 40 million immigrants, has multiplied sixfold to 175 million; the increase since 1940 alone has been 40 million. A half empty land has become the richest and most powerful nation on earth.

The centre of economic gravity is still in the north-east and Middle West, where basic industries first grew up within reach of rich fields of coal and iron ore. But newer developments have changed the economic and human map: oil in the south-west and California, minerals in the south and the Rockies, new industries on the Pacific coast and in the 'Old South'. The pre-war TVA plan, which rescued the Tennessee valley from poverty, has been followed by other great state enterprises, especially in the Far West, which have harnessed the rivers to enrich agriculture and supply power to new industries far from the coalfields.

The 'centre of gravity' of population, still creeping westwards, is now a little west of the Chicago–New Orleans line. The fastest growth of population is along the Pacific coast; there, about 20 million people will soon live where there were only 13 million in 1945. In the south-western plains, the pre-war 'dust bowl' has again been parched by seven years of drought; but this time the farmers have stayed on their land, helped by $500 million worth of state aid.

As important as the westward flow is the new movement of people between south and north. A generation ago the 'Old South' of cotton and tobacco was still a depressed area, and seemingly without hope of solving the problem of nine million Negroes who were mostly poor, socially segregated and politically without rights. Post-war progress, such as the ending of segregation in many southern schools, has been eased by migration as well as by more liberal thinking. (There have, however, been several notorious recent episodes revealing the southern whites' continued rejection of racial 'integration' in education and other spheres.) Today, less than two-thirds of the 16 million American Negroes live in the south. Two million have

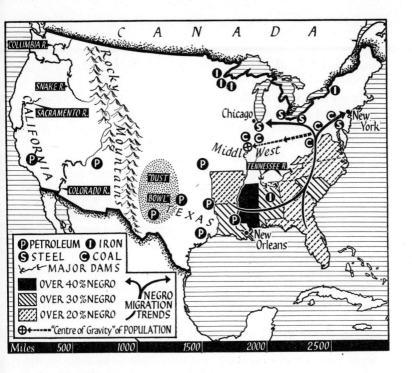

gone north, half a million to the Pacific coast, to work in new or growing industries. Only in one state, Mississippi—against six in 1900—do Negroes now exceed two-fifths of the population. Meanwhile northern whites and northern money have come south to help develop the new industrial and mining enterprises which have improved the lot of millions of Negroes and 'poor whites' alike.

67

LATIN AMERICA SEEKS LIBERTY

In 1959 the Cuban rebels' victory showed that the Latin Americans had almost got rid of the military dictators who had long ruled so many of the twenty republics. Only two outright military dictators retained power, in Paraguay and the Dominican Republic, though undemocratic regimes also survived rather shakily in other small states such as Nicaragua and Haiti. But the new surge of demands for liberty had brought down the 'strong men' one after another in a mere four years, and no major republic is now under dictatorial rule.

Argentina, in 1955, ousted General Peron, who had built up a fully totalitarian regime over twelve years. Peru's military dictator quietly handed over power in 1956; Colombia's was overthrown in 1957, Venezuela's early in 1958, and Cuba's a year later.

The formerly frequent United States interventions in the less stable Caribbean republics had been replaced in the 1930s by the 'good neighbour policy'. In the 1945 Act of Chapultepec, the 1947 Rio Treaty, and the 1948 Charter of the Organization of American States, the twenty republics and the U.S. pledged joint resistance to any outside attack on any one of them, and also undertook to try to settle any disputes between themselves before resorting to the United Nations. Some territorial disputes still recur—for instance, between Peru and Ecuador—but there has been no post-war clash comparable to the 1932–5 Chaco war between Bolivia and Paraguay.

The Latin Americans formally deplore the continued existence of colonial territories on their continent (there is less interest in the adjacent islands, which are hardly 'Latin', apart from Argentina's claim to the British Falklands (70)). But in practice none of the republics presses any claim to the Guianas, and support for Guatemala's claim to British Honduras (68) is lukewarm.

68

CARIBBEAN PATCHWORK

The patchwork look of Central America and the West Indies is partly geographical, partly the result of past colonizing activities. Cuba, the Dominican Republic, and the six little republics between Mexico and Colombia are all former Spanish colonies. Haiti, a Negro republic, freed itself from French rule in 1803. Puerto Rico (formerly Spanish) and some of the nearby Virgin Islands (purchased from Denmark) are now United States dependencies; while the other Caribbean islands have been for centuries in British, French, or Dutch hands, and their population is of very mixed, largely African, origin.

Oil and the Panama Canal (42) give the Caribbean strategic importance. Venezuela, Colombia, and Trinidad yield a sixth of the world's petroleum (3). The canal is not only a focal point of trade, but also enables the U.S. fleet to move between Atlantic and Pacific. The West Indies form a protective screen across the approaches to it, and in 1940 Britain granted, in return for war supplies, leases for U.S. defence bases to be built in several islands.

Two recent attempts have been made to simplify the political patchwork. The Central American republics have sought—particularly since the overthrow of a communist-influenced government in Guatemala in 1954—to draw together and form a union embracing nine million people (ten if Panama joins it). More solid progress toward unity has been made in the British West Indies, which, encouraged by Britain, had been discussing federation since 1945, with a view to becoming an independent Commonwealth nation. The Federation of the West Indies formally came into being in 1958. British Honduras and Guiana, the Virgin Islands and the Bahamas were unwilling to join it, partly from fear of being swamped by migrants from crowded Jamaica, which contains over half of the three million people of the new federation. Most British Caribbean dependencies already have internal self-government; but in British Guiana the new constitution of 1953 soon had to be suspended because the first elections were won by a party which quickly

showed that it aimed at a communist-style regime. British Honduras has repeatedly been claimed by Guatemala, which has, however, rejected British offers to take the matter to the International Court.

69

ARCTIC ADVANCES

In 1959 the admission of Alaska to be the 49th of the United States of America spotlighted the new importance of the Arctic—economic as well as military. The development of Alaska, northern Canada (65), Danish Greenland, and Norwegian Spitzbergen has been matched in the Soviet Arctic (the Russians also mine coal in Spitzbergen). Russia, controlling nearly half of the whole Arctic, has been able to use many thousands of political prisoners to open up northern Siberia. Its ships now ply right round the Siberian coast in the two-month ice-free season, and minerals and other Arctic products are also shipped south up rivers like the Yenisey and Lena. Soviet economic plans depend heavily on continuing this development.

Many airfields and landing places for aircraft equipped to land on water or ice are now maintained in the Arctic; and Russian, Canadian, and American radar and scientific observation posts are numerous, some of them established on masses of ice which drift slowly round the polar regions. In 1958 an American atom-powered submarine, the *Nautilus*, successfully travelled under the ice right across the Pole from Pacific to Atlantic. The Scandinavians, however, were the first in the field with normal passenger air services right across the Arctic, starting flights across Greenland to western American and Canada in 1954, and later introducing flights via Alaska to Japan. These routes, far shorter than the more familiar ones further south, provide vivid evidence of the way man's new mastery of the Arctic can serve peaceful as well as military purposes.

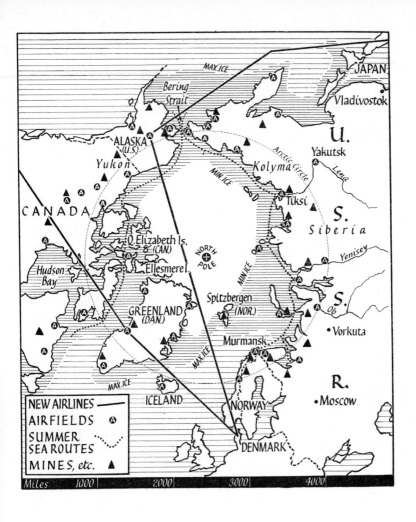

MAX.ICE

JAPAN

Bering
Strait

Vladivostok

ALASKA
(U.S.)

U.

Yakutsk

Yukon

Kolyma

MIN.ICE

Arctic Circle

Lena

CANADA

Tiksi

S.

Siberia

Q.Elizabeth Is.
(CAN.)

NORTH
POLE

Ellesmere I.

MIN.ICE

Yenisey

Hudson
Bay

Spitzbergen
(NOR.)

S.

Ob

GREENLAND
(DAN.)

Murmansk

Vorkuta

MAX.ICE

NORWAY

R.

MAX.ICE

ICELAND

DENMARK

Moscow

NEW AIRLINES ⎯⎯⎯
AIRFIELDS ⊛
SUMMER
SEA ROUTES ·····
MINES, etc. ▲

| Miles | 1000 | 2000 | 3000 | 4000 |

70

ANTARCTIC RIVALRY

The first land crossing of Antarctica, made in 1957-8 by the Commonwealth Trans-Antarctic Expedition, was part of the cooperative scientific effort of the International Geophysical Year. Any dramatic new discoveries made during the IGY activity are, however, obviously liable to intensify the international rivalry in Antarctica that has already grown up. Claims to sovereignty over sectors of the frozen continent's six million square miles have been made by Britain (1908), New Zealand (1923), Australia (1933), France (1924), and Norway (1939), all of whom recognize each others' claims; and by Chile (1940) and Argentina (1942), whose claims overlap with Britain's and with each other's. Since 1943 there has been occasional friction between Argentina, Chile, and Britain, but serious clashes have been avoided, partly by observance of an agreement reached in 1948 that no warships would be sent to the Antarctic. In 1947 Britain offered to bring the disputed claims before the International Court, but Argentina and Chile have never accepted this offer.

While the Argentine, Chilean, Australian, and New Zealand claims are based largely on propinquity, those of Britain and Norway arise mainly from long-established interests and activities. British sealing ships were working in what is now the Falkland Islands Dependencies, or British sector, in 1778. Modern whaling began there in 1906; police, customs, and magistrates have operated there since 1912. Norway has a long tradition of exploration (the South Pole was first reached by Amundsen in 1911) and today has the biggest whaling interest in the area.

America, Russia, and Japan, which all sent expeditions and set up bases for the Geophysical Year, claim no territory but do not recognize other countries' claims. The new American expeditions, like the many pre-war ones, have been most active in the unclaimed sector west of the British one and in New Zealand's Ross Dependency. The Russians have concentrated on the Australian sector. They have never before established an expedition in Antarctica, but since 1950 they have made play with a claim that a Russian admiral first sighted the continent in 1819 (though he did not recognize it to be the mainland); and they have insisted on having a voice in any discussion of its fate.

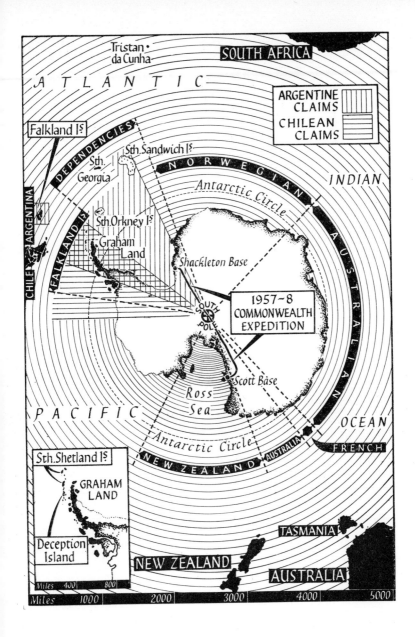

INDEX

The numbers refer to maps and accompanying notes, not to pages.
A number in bold type indicates a more detailed item.